★ THE BOOK OF ★
BASEBALL

★ ★ ★ ★ ★ ★ ★

★ ★ ★ ★ ★ ★

THE BOOK OF
BASEBALL

★ ★ ★ ★ ★ ★

in association with
SCOTTISH AMICABLE

★

by Derek Brandon
and Jim Marooney

★

SIDGWICK & JACKSON
LONDON

A Channel Four Book

★ ★ ★ ★ ★ ★

First published in Great Britain in 1987
by Sidgwick & Jackson Limited,
1 Tavistock Chambers, Bloomsbury Way, London WC1A 2SG
Copyright © 1987
by Derek Brandon and Jim Marooney

ISBN 0-283-99551-3

The Book of Baseball is associated with
Channel Four Television's coverage of the sport produced by
Cheerleader Productions Limited.

Edited, designed and produced by Swallow Books,
Swallow House, 11-21 Northdown Street, London N1 9BN

Designer: Jacqueline Palmer
Editor: Peter Arnold
Illustrator: David Dragon

Typeset in Great Britain by Wordbase Limited
Printed in Italy by Amilcare Pizzi s.p.a. Milan

Acknowledgements

The publishers wish to thank the following organisations for their
help in the preparation of this book. We apologise to anyone
we may have omitted to mention.

Allsport i, iii, 8, 10, 11, 16t, 16i, 18, 29, 30, 32r, 37, 42/3, 46, 47, 47i, 50/1, 57c, 62, 64b, 65, 73, 75, 85, 113: Simon
Brury 38/ Alvin Chung 91/ Tim de Frisco 119, 120i/ Brian Drake 109/ Tony Duffy 21, 54/ Jerry
Edler 77/ John Hayt 14, 15, 36i, 80, 96/ Thearon Henderson 69i/ T. G. Higgins 28r, 63, 71, 101, 103, 104,
107/ Trevor Jones 67i/ F. Kaplan 67r/ Caryn Levy 98/ Gray Mortimore 122, 123/ Mike Powell 57t,
59, 60/1, 93, 115/ Steve Powell 33b/ Larry Stoidt 41l/ L. Stout 69r, 83, 87, 88, 95, 111, 120/ Paul J.
Sutton 7/ S. Sutton 19/ Budd Symes 32t, 58/ Vandystadt 34/5; National Baseball Library, Cooperstown,
New York 17, 28l, 39t, 40, 41r, 43i, 47b, 55, 56t: Carl Seid 56b/ Ernie Sisto 31

t = top, b = bottom, l = left, r = right, i = inset

CONTENTS

FOREWORD

My first visit to the United States was in 1974. West Germany had just become football's World Champions, and I had never heard of a World Series.

I flew to the West Coast to stay with friends near Salinas, the part of America made famous by the writings of John Steinbeck – and I did get to see Cannery Row!

A chance hour spent in front of my host's television changed much of the itinerary of this particular tourist. Baseball was on, and I was hooked, instantly.

All I can remember about that first game I saw was that it was in New York and the pitcher was called Andy Messersmith. I well recall, however, bombarding my host with questions, the last of which was: 'When do we go to a major league game?'

My pals could take baseball or leave it, and probably they believed they'd bred a monster! But I was humoured by a trip to Oakland Coliseum. The Athletics were then the sport's hottest property. Stars like the young Reggie Jackson had catapulted the club to World Series victories. Watching in the flesh sharpened my appetite for the game.

When I returned to England, I mentioned how much I'd enjoyed baseball to an ITV Sport colleague, Derek Brandon, then editor of Granada Television's Friday night football preview programme *Kick-off*.

Derek must be blessed with a good memory because eleven years later he asked me to present a baseball programme for Channel 4. By now he had started his own company, Cheerleader Productions. The following year we put together seven programmes covering the play-offs and the World Series – and on behalf of the Channel 4 viewers I was able to ask major league heroes like Gary Carter and Dwight Evans those questions I'd first asked a decade earlier.

I was very pleased that Derek too was attracted to the game, an attraction which has led to the writing of this book. If like the two of us you've been bitten by the baseball bug, then you will enjoy this book – if you are a 'don't know', then I'm sure it will make a fan of you.

Martin Tyler

New York celebrates the Mets' 1986 World Series victory.

★ ★ ★ ★ ★ ★

INTRODUCTION

★ ★ ★ ★ ★ ★

Now that American football claims increasing attention from the marketing men and the television moguls, the American people have returned to baseball as their own favourite sporting pastime. Baseball has always been very much the sport of the people because it is much more accessible – tickets are easier and cheaper to acquire and if you live in one of the big cities like New York, Chicago or Los Angeles you can catch a game most days during the season. Television's new super-stations beam games of what were once regional teams – the New York Yankees and Mets, the Chicago Cubs and the Atlanta Braves – right across the country, and sports fans of both sexes follow baseball in a way that is unique in America and hard to imagine in Britain.

The hesitation in bringing America's great summer sport to British television audiences lies in Channel 4 not wishing to appear an American-dominated sports channel and in the fact that baseball is a sport which undoubtedly requires a lot of concentration from the audience. But now that we have taken the plunge, we fully expect to develop a very substantial following on this side of the Atlantic. Baseball is a subtle sport which may not have the immediate hit-you-between-the-eyes impact of American football, but for many people it is a much more satisfying game, possessing a natural pace which ebbs and flows across the three or so hours of most games.

Baseball is a sport which richly rewards a little concentration spent on it and we hope this book, together with the 'idiots' guides' that we regularly feature in the Channel 4 programmes, will help the British audience appreciate this most wonderful of sports. We have not attempted a full-scale manual which explains every situation which might occur on a baseball fiield. There are hundreds of complex rules which rival the laws of cricket in incomprehension to an absolute newcomer, most of them covering very rare situations. Our aim has been to reveal enough of the game and the teams who play it to enable viewers to follow the play and pick up the subtleties as they go along.

Much of the anecdotal material comes from Jim Marooney, Cheerleader's New York-based producer. He has covered baseball for American networks from every one of the 26 stadiums in the major leagues.

We would like to thank Martin Tyler for his foreword to this book, Chiz Dube for master-minding the production of the manuscript, Susanna Yager at Channel 4 (the book's mid-wife), the editorial and production teams for agreeing to impossible deadlines, Scottish Amicable Life Assurance Society who sponsor the sport in the UK, and Adrian Metcalfe at Channel 4 for ten hours of Channel 4 airtime which should allow us capture all the excitement of the play-offs and World Series.

Derek Brandon and Jim Marooney

Darryl Strawberry of the New York Mets beats the ball back to home base for a run against the Los Angeles Dodgers.

★ ★ ★ ★ ★ ★

BASEBALL
★ ★ BASICS ★ ★

No, baseball is not the same as rounders. There are some obvious similarities but anybody who has had a hard ball thrown just past his nose at over 90 mph knows what playing baseball is like.

American professional ballplayers play a daunting schedule of 162 games from April through to September, six months in which they live together on planes and in hotel rooms in a marathon that puts more sporting and social pressure on a player than any other sport except perhaps professional basketball. Baseball is tough physically, mentally and emotionally.

However, the rewards are great too, and the sport is firmly established in America as the country's favourite pastime.

The central part of a baseball arena is its diamond-shaped infield. The four points of the diamond, which are 90 feet apart, are known as home plate, first base, second base and third base. The objective for the team at bat is to advance the batter to each of the bases, hoping that he will come round to complete a run. This principle is, of course, the same as in rounders.

The Jack Murphy Stadium of the San Diego Padres, which seats 58,433.

The batter can move around the bases one at a time, by scoring what are called base hits, or he can go in bigger leaps. Hitting the ball far enough for him to reach first base safely is a base hit, or single. If he can safely round first base to second he scores a double. Sometimes, but not often, the batter will have the time to run all the way round the diamond to third base and will record a triple. Not that he will actually score anything on the scoreboard for that, because he will have to get all the way round to home plate before he records a run for his side. The next man at bat will hope to hit at least a single to allow the man at third base to come home and record a run to the batting team.

Some hits bring greater reward than others. The quickest and most dramatic way to score is to hit the ball over the perimeter fence within fair territory and score a home run. Fair territory is between the foul lines which run from home plate past first and third bases. In other words the ball must be hit in front of the batter to count. A home run is sure to bring the crowd to its feet. Roughly similar to a six in cricket, but even more significant, the home run allows the batter to score immediately, and for everyone on base ahead of him to score too. So a home run scored with the bases loaded, i.e. with men at first, second and third bases, scores not one but four runs for the team (a grand slam).

ABOVE RIGHT: **Jump as high as you can, but if that ball goes over the fence, it's a home run.**

RIGHT: **The ball caught 'on the fly', i.e. without bouncing, puts the batter out.**

The aim of the fielding team is to prevent such scoring, and they use nine players. The pitcher, the catcher, a first baseman, second baseman, third baseman and a short stop all guard the infield. In the outfield, more than a hundred yards from the batter, are a left fielder, center fielder and right fielder.

The essence of the game is the confrontation between the pitcher and the batter. The pitcher hurls the ball with speed and swerve at around 90 mph from his mound just 20 yards away from the batter. The pitcher is generally aiming to throw the ball into the strike zone, which is an imaginary box of the width of the home plate and directly above it. The bottom of the box is level with the batter's knees and the top of the box with his chest. If the ball misses the strike zone and the batter does not swing at it the umpire behind the catcher will call the pitch 'a ball'. But if the pitch is in the strike zone and the batter doesn't swing, or if he swings and misses any pitch, the umpire will call 'strike'.

Left Field

Umpire

Third Base

Third Base Coach

THE STRIKE ZONE

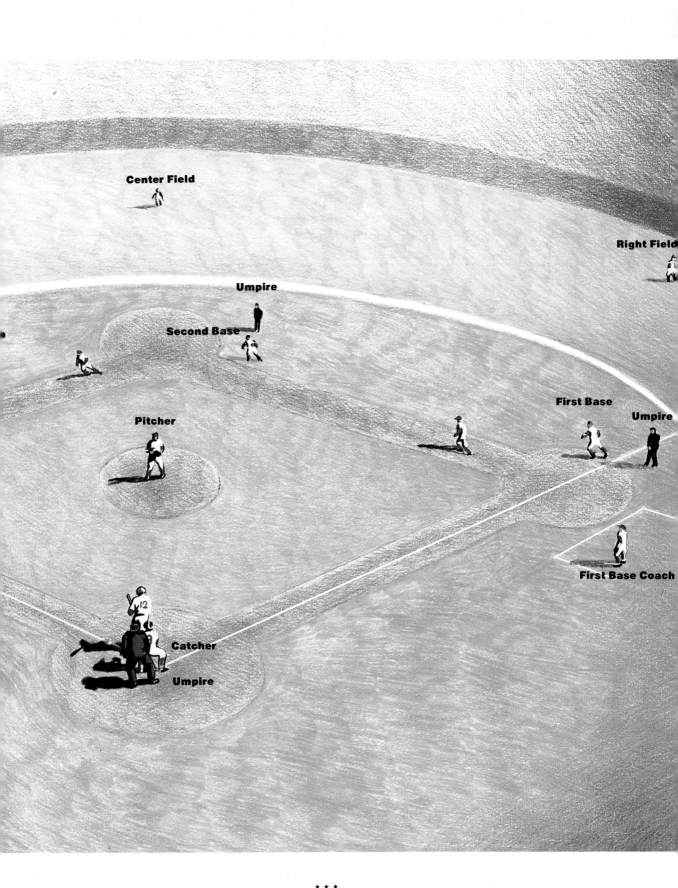

This is the fundamental thing to learn about baseball: four balls and the batter walks to first base; three strikes and he is out.

When the batter does make contact, just as in cricket, he is out if the ball is caught on the full (called in baseball being caught 'on the fly'). He's also out if a fielder gets to a base before him with the ball, or if a fielder touches him ('tags him out') with it. A batter who hits must run.

In baseball the home team always bats second, giving it the advantage of not having to bat the last half-inning if it has already won the game. The whole squad of players can take part in a game; as in all American sports there is unlimited substitution, the only proviso in baseball being that once a player has been replaced by a substitute he cannot return to the game. Substitute, or relief, pitchers are specialists who concentrate on winning or saving games and are not normally starters.

Each member of the batting side comes up in rotation until three outs are recorded, that being the end of the inning. There are nine innings in a game, and if the score is tied at the end of nine innings extra innings are played until there is a result. Although there is considerable variation, the average major league game lasts about three hours.

Baseball combines individual initiative with team understanding. It's a game which tests the player's agility, strength, speed and stamina and can lift the emotions of players and fans alike to the heights of exhilaration.

Balls, strikes, hits and runs are the components from which is made the compelling game of baseball.

The left-hander Holland pitching for Pittsburgh (he later moved to the New York Yankees).

THE UMPIRES

Four umpires officiate in major league base-ball games, except in play-offs and the World Series, when two more are added to the crew. The chief 'honcho' is at home plate; he calls the balls and strikes and the close calls when a runner heads for home. The other umpires are at each of the bases and their prime role is to judge whether a runner beats a throw to his base. The additional two umpires in post-season games patrol the lines drawn from home plate to first and third bases.

Umpires are expected to listen to appeals from managers up to a certain point. If an appeal becomes too heated they have the power to eject the offender from the game. Questioning an umpire's ancestry is one good way to be ejected;

even baseball's only deaf-mute pitcher managed to get himself sent off once for cursing at an umpire in sign language.

Umpires earn between $30,000 and $80,000 a season and are on the road all the time – there are no home games for umpires. Baseball lore has it that if someone has three strikes on you, the best lawyer in America can't get you off. The umpire Bill Guthrie put it more simply: 'Der ain't no close plays, me lad; dey is either dis or dat.' Another umpire's philosophy has always been: 'Call 'em fast and walk away tough.' It is claimed that umpiring major league baseball is one of the most stressful occupations you can have – on a par with air traffic controllers and big city policemen.

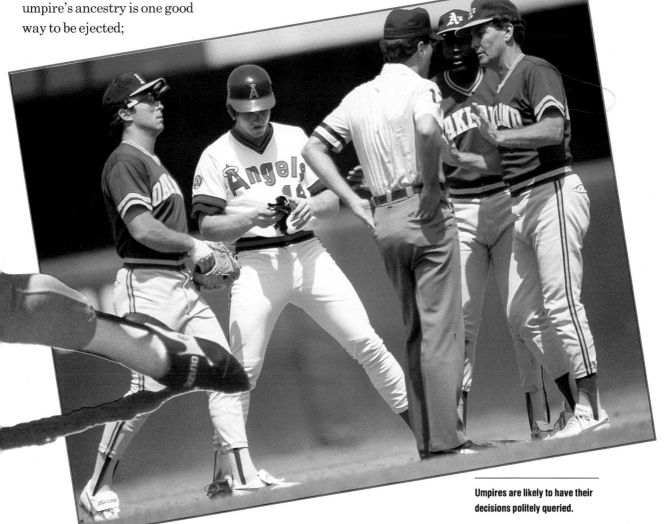

Umpires are likely to have their decisions politely queried.

THE COACHES

There is a story in cricket that when W.G. Grace was once bowled out first ball he calmly picked up the bail, returned it to the stumps and said: 'Don't be ridiculous all these good people have come to see me bat!' In baseball Babe Ruth had less success with the same strategy: 'There's 40,000 people here who know that last one was a ball, tomato-head!' On this occasion the umpire replied: 'Maybe so, but mine is the only opinion that counts.'

ABOVE: The base umpire has to decide who's first, batter or ball.

RIGHT: Connie Mack, founder and manager of the Philadelphia Athletics.

As in all American sports there are a number of specialist baseball coaches. The head coach is the manager, who selects the line-up and is responsible for strategy on game day. On the field of play, while a side is batting, will be a first base coach, who will advise a runner on that base, especially on stealing second, and will be in the eyeline of the batter, and a third base coach who advises by arm signals whether a runner should stop at third or head for home plate. Behind the scenes are pitching and batting coaches. All baseball coaches wear the team's uniform (except for the famous Connie Mack who owned the team as well and therefore felt able to sit in the dug-out wearing a suit!) and they have their own numbers.

PITCHING

★ ★ ★ ★ ★ ★

There are three basic pitches in baseball, although every pitcher has his own variations on the main themes: the fastball, the curveball and the slider. Each can be made by either a left-handed pitcher or a right-handed pitcher, making six basic techniques which throw up different problems for the batter. The **fastball** is what its name suggests – a delivery hurled by the pitcher with as much speed as he can muster. A **curveball** dips down just as it reaches the batter, while a **slider** is equally hard to play, moving across the batter and dropping away at the same time.

There are of course other pitches. You may hear of a **knuckleball,** an almost extinct pitch which is so unpredictable catchers find it almost impossible to get their glove to them. One catcher says they're not that difficult though: 'I just wait till they stop rolling and then pick them up!' A **forkball** was an antecedent of the split-fingered fastball, now not seen. A **screwball** is a curveball that moves away from the batter's body.

Illegal pitches are the **'spitball'** in which a globule of saliva makes the ball unstable in the air, and its close relative the **scuffball,** in which sandpaper is applied to the ball to roughen it on one side and again create an unpredictability in its passage through the air.

Pitchers can be left-handed or right-handed (and once in a while one comes along who can be both) and are used tactically against batting sides that are filled with left- or right-handers. Normally lefties fare better against lefties so both sides will vary their line-ups to take advantage (once out of a game, a pitcher is not allowed to return). Even during a game a manager may take out his pitcher to bring in another one whose left-handedness may give his side the edge against the next batter or series of batters. Baseballers play the percentages and a change to a left-handed pitcher can load the dice in the fielding team's favour. As one manager put it: 'However good you are, you are going to lose 54 games a season; however bad you are, you are going to win 54 games a season. It's the other 54 games that decide whether you're still going to be in a job next year!'

Pitchers put such stress on their arms that it is unusual to pitch more than about six innings in a game, say 100-120 pitches. Then they are re-placed (relieved) and are literally put on ice for three or four days. The pitching motion bends the elbow back on itself and it really does take three days for the arm to recover. Ice-packs and sometimes manipulation are necessary to keep the pitcher fit. Teams have a squad of around ten pitchers – some specialise in starting games, some are specialist 'relievers', some are defensive specialists used to 'close out' a tight game. Some are used for their left- (or right-) hand-edness against a line-up strong on left- (or right-) handers.

A good pitcher (here, the Mets' Dwight Gooden) whips the ball forward from a bent elbow and keeps his body low as he hurtles round.

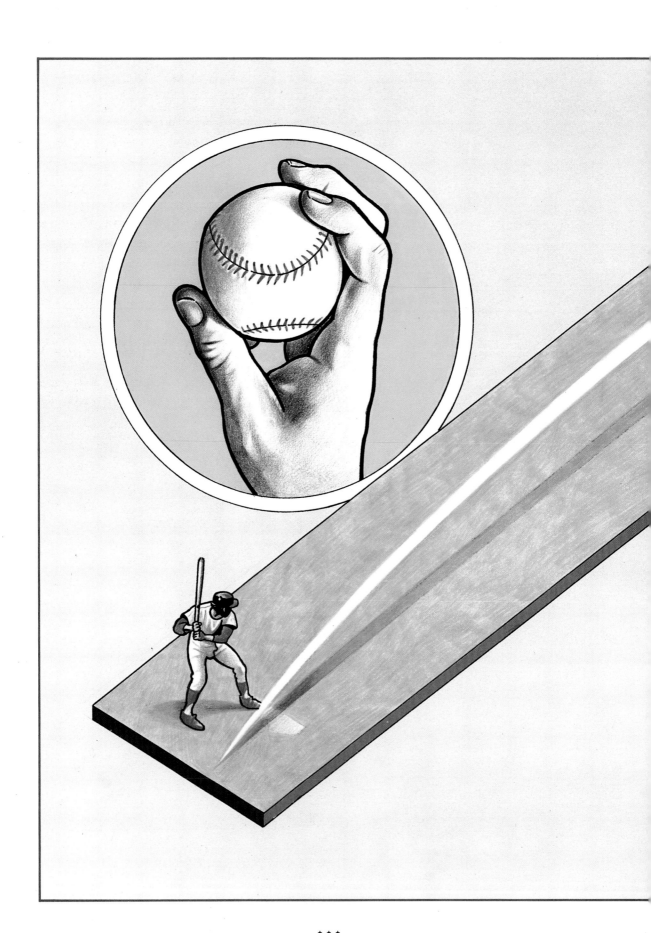

THE FASTBALL

THE FASTBALL

The fastball more or less speaks for itself. Thrown at the strike zone at speeds of around 95 mph, it takes just half a second to reach the batter – half a second for him to decide whether to swing at it, and, if he does, to produce the swing which he hopes will carry the ball over the fence for a home run. Thrown at those speeds, the ball makes a distinctive noise as it travels through the air. The batter, reading the state of the game and counting the pitches, will frequently guess the pitcher's intentions and will swing down the line of the fastball and hope for the best. For a fastball, the ball is held with the index and forefingers bissecting the seams at top and bottom. The fastest pitch ever recorded, by the way, was of 108 mph, and was thrown by Nolan Ryan in 1974.

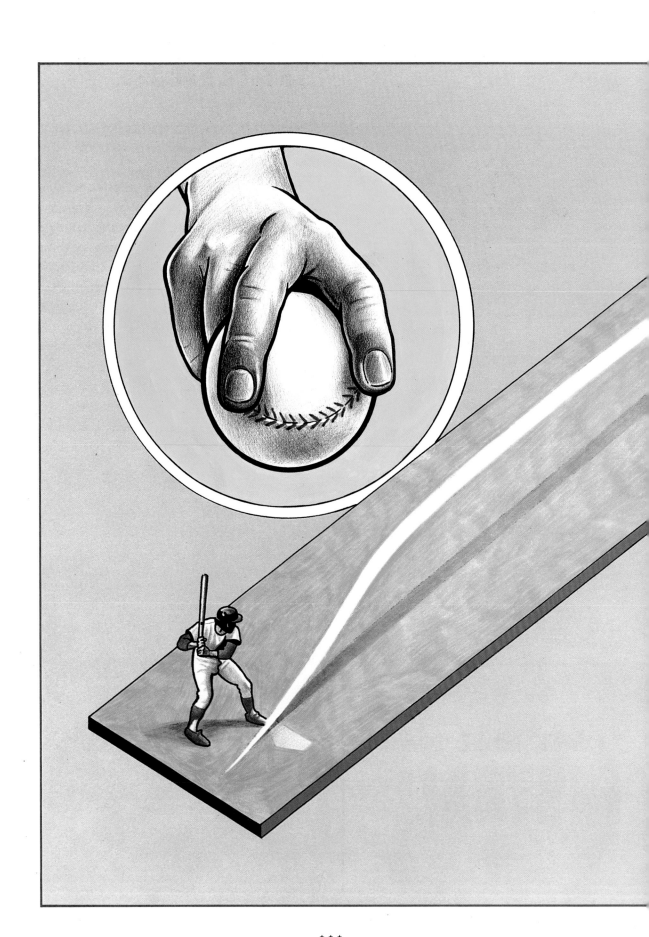

THE SPLIT-FINGERED FASTBALL

A recent variation of the fastball (which caused some devastation among batters in 1986 and will probably cause even more damage to batting statistics in 1987 as more and more pitchers perfect its rather difficult technique) is the split-fingered fastball. This is just as fast but because of the different grip, the ball dips wickedly at the last moment as it passes over the plate, producing a virtually unplayable pitch – baseball's equivalent, if you like, of cricket's fast yorker.

When perfecting the split-fingered fastball the pitcher keeps moving his index and fore-fingers down the sides of the ball. He keeps moving them down until it gets too uncomfortable to hold the ball. It's the pressure applied to the sides of the ball which causes it to drop like a stone over the plate.

★★ T H E ★★
SPLIT-FINGERED
FASTBALL

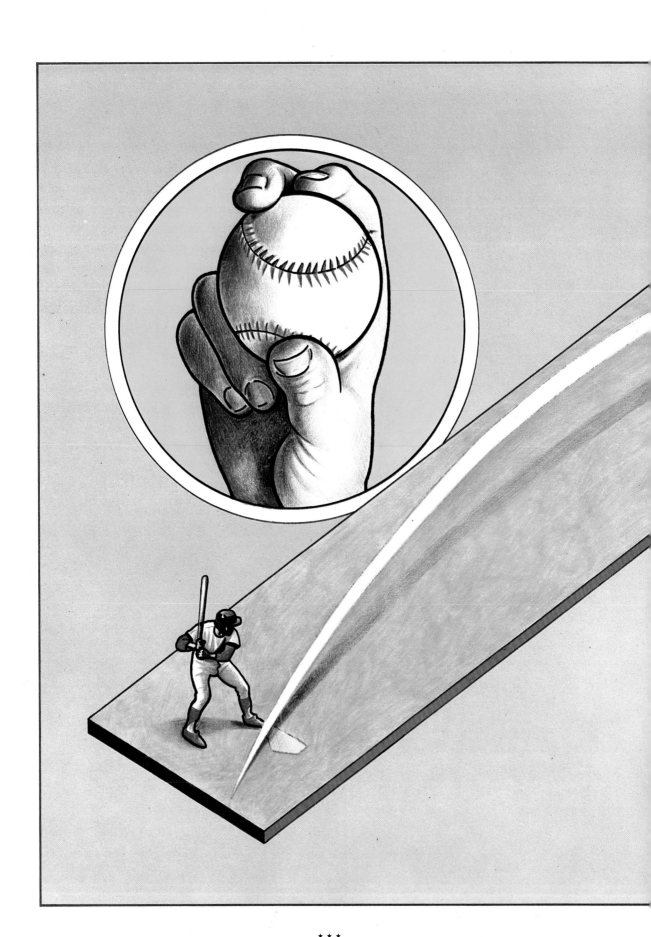

THE CURVEBALL

The curveball dips as it crosses the plate, making it difficult for the batter to judge whether the pitch is a ball or a strike. The grip is the same as a fastball but the fingers are parallel with the seam. Remember that the pitcher adjusts his grip behind the glove out of sight of the batter! A Dodgers pitcher named Whitlow Wyatt was once told that scientists were claiming that a curveball was only an optical illusion. Wyatt offered to prove it wasn't. 'Stand a scientist behind a tree and I'll womp him to death with an optical illusion,' he said.

★★ THE ★★
CURVEBALL

★ THE ★
SLIDER

THE SLIDER

The slider moves across the plate as well as dipping, baseball's equivalent of the outswinger (or inswinger) in cricket. It's particularly effective because it appears to be a fastball but then tails away at the last split second. The ball is held in a similar grip to the curveball, only more tightly and slightly off centre.

BATTING

★ ★ ★ ★ ★ ★

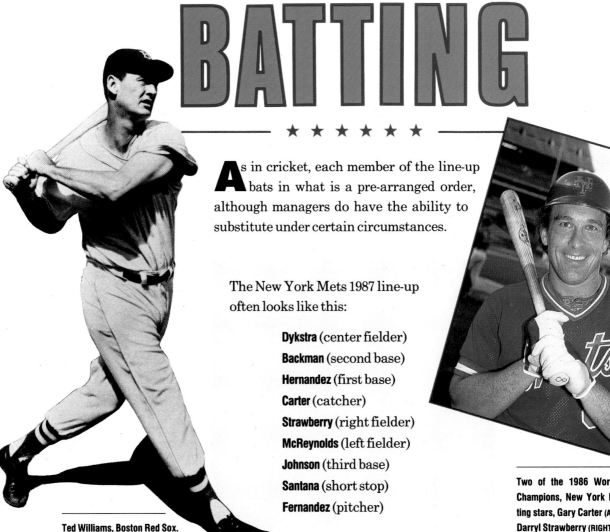

As in cricket, each member of the line-up bats in what is a pre-arranged order, although managers do have the ability to substitute under certain circumstances.

The New York Mets 1987 line-up often looks like this:

Dykstra (center fielder)
Backman (second base)
Hernandez (first base)
Carter (catcher)
Strawberry (right fielder)
McReynolds (left fielder)
Johnson (third base)
Santana (short stop)
Fernandez (pitcher)

Ted Williams, Boston Red Sox.

Two of the 1986 World Series Champions, New York Mets batting stars, Gary Carter (ABOVE) and Darryl Strawberry (RIGHT).

The batting line-up is carefully designed to give the Mets the best chance to capitalise on the strengths of their players. By opening up with two reliable batters in Dykstra and Backman the Mets reckon to get at least one man on base before the big hitters Hernandez, Carter and Strawberry come to the plate. If all goes well a big hit from one of these three will make contact for a multiple score. The batting line-up also ensures, mostly, a strong opening to the second inning after three outs have been recorded to end the first (because in baseball, the first batter in each inning is the batter who would have batted next in the previous inning had the side not been out).

There are two major leagues in American pro baseball, the American League and the National League, and in the American League pitchers don't bat. Each team carries an extra batter (who does not take his place on the field) who is brought into the line-up as a 'designated hitter'. Ageing stars like Reggie Jackson keep their careers going for a few more seasons by playing as a 'dh'. In World Series games, where the American League champions play the National League champions, the rules of the home club are played, so designated hitters play in games at the home of the American League club but are not allowed to play in games at the home of the National League club.

In both leagues a weaker batter can be replaced by a substitute in the batting order, known as a 'pinch hitter'. However, in this case the man who has been replaced cannot play any further part in the game. This rule is frequently used to bring an extra batter into play shortly before changing pitchers, the pitcher being taken out of the batting rotation (and therefore out of the game) and replaced by a batting specialist.

THE BAT & BALL

THE BAT

The original flat-sided bats were changed to the now familiar round bats in 1893. To a Brit brought up on cricket, the bat appears to be a little unwieldy, and although it weighs 30-36 ounces compared to say 40-50 ounces for a professional cricketer's bat, it feels heavy because it is wielded at shoulder height. Baseball bats are about 36 inches long, and taper to a thinner handle. Only the first 18 inches of the handle can be treated with sticky stuff (usually pine tar) to help the batter's grip. Bats are not sprung, as cricket bats are, and a base hit is felt right through the body, although there is perhaps a much more satisfying 'crack' when a big contact is made by a baseball bat.

The wood used is white ash, as many as 60 bats being fashioned from one 50-year-old tree. In a typical major league game two or three bats will be broken by contact with the ball, the more muted crack sound still being audible from the stands. Add in practice, and players get through between six and eight dozen bats *each* in a season.

Players often warm up with a lead 'doughnut' over the end of the bat – usually using it in the on-deck circle just before they come to bat. This has the effect of making the bat feel lighter when the doughnut is removed, as it must be, when they go to the plate.

A rack of bats belonging to the Mets and Reds at Shea Stadium.

THE BALL

The ball, always white with heavy red stitching, is leather and weighs about five ounces, approximately the same as a cricket ball. The seams protrude in a similar fashion, but in a different pattern, to those on a cricket ball. Since 1910 baseballs have had cork centres, around which yarn is wound. This is covered with two strips of leather sewn together tightly. Horsehide was used until 1975 when cowhide was introduced due to a shortage of horses!

The ball is softer and less highly polished than a cricket ball, in fact umpires rub balls in a special mud before a game to remove excess shine. Unlike in cricket, where a ball is expected to last 85 overs with bowlers making use of the changing characteristics of an ageing ball, a baseball is usually hit only once before it is rejected (or taken home as a souvenir by a fan if it lands in the stands). Thus over 100,000 balls are used in the two major leagues during a season. They are made by Rawlings, who supply each club with 15,000 balls a season at a cost of $3 each (compared to a retail cost of about $12 each). This totals over half a million balls every year. Sixty balls in sealed packets are supplied to umpires before each game.

Joe DiMaggio of the New York Yankees, one of three baseballing brothers and one of the sport's greatest names in the 1940s and 50s.

THE
FIELDING
★ SIDE ★

A fielder wears the distinctive leather catching glove on the end of his weaker arm. Whereas in cricket it is not uncommon for a catch to be dropped, in baseball, the catcher, because of the glove, is expected to catch the ball if it goes anywhere near him. The ball is taken in the glove, and transferred to the other, stronger hand for throwing. At the highest level, catches can be spectacular, the throwing to bases blistering, and the speed of thought involved in, say, a double play (where two runners are thrown out in one play) can seem bewildering to the uninitiated.

Until 1954, fielders dropped their gloves on the ground where they stood at the end of an inning, and the other side had to negotiate their way around this minefield of obstacles when they fielded, which added to the excitement and unpredictability of the game, but not, perhaps, in the best way.

RIGHT: A runner's foot anchored on base in readiness to run.

ABOVE RIGHT: Catcher's mitt with a Pittsburgh Pirates cap.

FAR RIGHT: The Mets' Mookie Wilson waiting in the outfield.

CATCHING

The catcher, who wears a heavier glove than the fielders, does much more than represent baseball's equivalent of cricket's wicketkeeper, although he does also have to catch balls which pass the batter. Just as the first violin acts as orchestra leader for a conductor, so the catcher leads the fielding team. Although the final decision on what sort of pitch is to be thrown rests with the pitcher himself, the catcher generally makes a suggestion based on his knowledge of the batter and the situation at that moment. The value of the catcher in this respect is that he plays most days of the season and builds up an encyclopaedic knowledge of the strengths and weaknesses of individual batsmen. Pitchers play at most once in a three- or four-game series and so often rely on the catcher's information. The catcher will signal to the pitcher with signs made down by his groin as he crouches behind the plate, and thus hidden from other players' view. The usual signals are one finger for a fastball, two fingers for a curveball, and three fingers for a slider.

Sometimes a catcher might make a whole series of signals if he suspects someone else is watching – only he and the pitcher will know which signal is the real one.

An indication of the catcher's worth to a team is given by the highest paid player for the Mets. He's Gary Carter, the catcher, who is paid $2 million a year.

BELOW: Rob Wilfong makes a difficult stop look easy.

BOTTOM: The catcher has to be ready to catch a strike.

PUTTING OUT
BATTERS & RUNNERS

The principal ways in which the fielding side can put out the batting side are as follows:

a) by catching a ball which the batter hits on the fly (i.e. by catching it before it bounces). This puts out the batter.

b) by causing the batter to fail to make contact with three strikes (providing the catcher catches the third strike). This also puts out the batter.

c) by 'tagging' a runner, i.e. by a fielder with the ball touching a runner before the runner reaches the base. This puts out the runner.

d) by a fielder's touching a base while holding the ball when the runner has not reached the base but is forced to run on because another runner is running to the previous base which he occupied.

A double play occurs when two outs are made on the same pitch, for instance a runner on first base might be forced out at second if the batter hits the ball to the second baseman, and a quick throw of the ball to first base might also force the batter. A triple play could occur if a catch was also involved with two tags. A triple play automatically ends the inning, as it puts three men out.

Batters and runners can also be out for infringements of the laws about interfering with the fielders.

Much of the most exciting action in baseball happens around the bases, as the runners sprint, slide, and fall to reach them before the ball gets to the baseman (INSET). Whether the runner is out or not, the baseman can still throw to another base in the hope of getting another runner out (RIGHT).

HOW ★★ IT ALL BEGAN

Even the Americans have to admit that baseball is essentially a British sport. Eighteenth-century immigrants from the Old Country brought over rounders – basically a children's game, of course – although the game has been much changed over the years.

You will find it written that the sport of baseball was invented by Abner Doubleday in Cooperstown, New York – home today of the Baseball Hall of Fame. This claim is total nonsense – baseball was being played in New England long before Doubleday was around.

The first set of rules for the improved American version of baseball was drawn up in 1845 by one Alexander Cartwright, founder of the Knickerbocker Base Ball Club in New York.

These rules, which were widely adopted throughout the region, established the shape of the present diamond with its home plate and the three other bases. Further modifications to the rules were made in New York in 1858 and 1863. Oddly, the biggest single factor

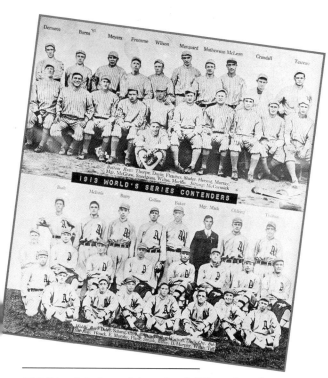

ABOVE: Team photos have not changed much. This one shows the Philadelphia Athletics (lower team) who beat the New York Giants in the 1913 World Series.

in spreading the sport of baseball throughout the United States was Civil War in the 1860s: soldiers from the north took the sport into the deep south.

The Cincinnati Red Stockings became the first professional club in 1869. Interestingly this was seven years after the formation of the oldest Football League club, Notts County, but was sixteen years ahead of professionalism being legalised in football.

The first major league was formed in 1876: the National League. The then rival American League was formed in 1900, largely by teams who could not get into the older league.

Baseball has become a truly international game being played in over 60 countries and with professional leagues in Japan and throughout the Caribbean area. It has achieved the status of exhibition sport at the 1988 Olympic Games at Seoul and will become a medal sport at the 1992 Olympics at Barcelona.

Baseball has been played in Britain since Victorian times and Britain, in fact, won the world amateur championship in 1938. Many of the early clubs were linked to football teams (hence Derby County's Baseball Ground). The sport declined in popularity after the war, but is now enjoying a resurgence, with the formation in 1987 of a formally run National League, backed by Scottish Amicable Life Assurance Society. The League is starting with six teams – Humberside County Bears, Nottingham Knights, London Warriors, Southern Tigers, Lancashire Red Sox and Mersey Mariners. There are now over 100 clubs organised by the British Baseball Federation and baseball is bound to grow in Britain. The writers and publishers of this book wish everyone connected with the League great success.

LEFT: The game is spreading in the UK, both informally, as in this game in London's Regent's Park, and in the National League sponsored by the Scottish Amicable Life Assurance Society.

THE LEAGUES

There were originally two quite independent and rival leagues, the National and the American. The two leagues are still independently run but are no longer rivals, and together they make up major league baseball.

There are two divisions of each league, made up as follows:

Some of the stars of the National League: (ABOVE) Ernie Banks of the Chicago Cubs, with the ball he hit for his 500th home run in 1970; (LEFT) Pee Wee Reese of the Brooklyn Dodgers.

AMERICAN LEAGUE

EAST DIVISION	WEST DIVISION
Baltimore Orioles	California Angels
Boston Red Sox	Chicago White Sox
Cleveland Indians	Kansas City Royals
Detroit Tigers	Minnesota Twins
Milwaukee Brewers	Oakland Athletics
New York Yankees	Seattle Mariners
Toronto Blue Jays	Texas Rangers

NATIONAL LEAGUE

EAST DIVISION	WEST DIVISION
Chicago Cubs	Atlanta Braves
Montreal Expos	Cincinnati Reds
New York Mets	Houston Astros
Philadelphia Phillies	Los Angeles Dodgers
Pittsburgh Pirates	San Diego Padres
St Louis Cardinals	San Francisco Giants

Unlike in the National Football League, there is no inter-conference play in baseball except in the World Series. Clubs play games against the other clubs in both divisions of their own league but not against clubs from the other league.

LEFT: **Mike Scott of the Houston Astros, master of the split-fingered fasball; and (BELOW) Rogers Hornsby of the St Louis Cardinals, National League's batting champion for a record six years, 1920-25.**

NATIONAL LEAGUE

The senior of the two leagues both in age and, to most Americans, in status too, the National League was founded in 1876, the eight charter members being the Chicago White Stockings, St Louis, Cincinnati, Louisville, Philadelphia, Boston, Hartford and New York. Boston beat Philadelphia 6-5 in the first NL game – and major league baseball really dates back to that game played on 22 April 1876.

The National League stayed pretty much as it started until 1953 when the Boston Braves, having been refused a move to the West Coast, were allowed to move to Milwaukee. At that time the major population growth areas were in California, and baseball owners were keen to move from the fading east to the rising west. In 1958 New York baseball fans suffered two shattering blows when not just one but both the city's National League teams left and headed for California. The Brooklyn Dodgers took what turned out to be the plum by moving to Los Angeles, the New York Giants took the lemon, although they thought they had taken the best option, when they moved to San Francisco. New York survived until 1962 without a National League team. In that year, the New York Mets were formed and took their place in the league along with another new team the Houston Colt 45s (later known as the Astros). In 1966 the Milwaukee, née Boston, Braves moved down to Atlanta, and in 1969 two new franchises were awarded to San Diego and Montreal (which became the first major league club from Canada).

The natural conservatism of the older league was well summed up by Edward Bennett

Williams, owner of the American League Baltimore Orioles: 'National League owners are 100 per cent for progress and 100 per cent against change.'

In the National League of twelve teams, each club plays nine games at home and nine games away against each of the clubs in its own division, and six at home and six away against clubs in the other division.

AMERICAN LEAGUE

The American League began as a confederation of clubs who couldn't get into the well-established National League. The main impetus came in 1900 when Chicago, Boston and Philadelphia were joined by Detroit, Baltimore, Washington, Cleveland and Milwaukee to form the American League.

Some people think that the removal of whole franchises to another city is a recent development thought up by NFL owners, but baseball has suffered from and profited from the transplanting of clubs to other cities for a long time. After St Louis replaced Milwaukee in 1903, the Baltimore franchise was moved to New York. Eventually, in 1954, the St Louis Browns were moved to Baltimore and the following year Kansas City became the new home of the Philadelphia Athletics. The Washington Senators became the Minnesota Twins in 1961, and new franchises were awarded to Washington and Los Angeles with the establishment of the California Angels and a new Washington Senators team. Seven years later the Athletics made their second move, this time to Oakland, and in 1969 new franchises were picked up by Kansas City (now the Royals) and the West Coast city of Seattle.

After just one year in Seattle the club moved to Milwaukee in 1970, and in 1972 the Washington club became the Texas Rangers. Toronto and a new Seattle club joined the league in 1977.

The American League is still seen as the junior partner of the two leagues but innovations like the designated hitter seem to come more naturally to the newcomers than to the old guard of the National League.

In the fourteen-team American League each club plays twelve games (six at home and six away) against all thirteen opponents – a total of 156 games. Each club then plays an additional six games, three at home and three away, with teams from its own division. This makes a regular season's total of 162 games.

TOP: The Indians' Napoleon Lajoie and (ABOVE) Detroit's Ty Cobb.

ABOVE: Roger Clemens, who was the Red Sox top pitcher in 1986.

MAIN PICTURE: National League 1985 play-offs, the Dodgers v. the Cardinals.

THE PLAY-OFFS

At the end of the regular season there is a champion of each of the two divisions in each league. There then follows the League Championship Series in each league. These are, if you like, World Series semi-finals.

The League Championship Series (known as the LCS) is played over a best-of-seven format which throws up champions of the American League and the National League. It is these two champions who play-off for the World Series.

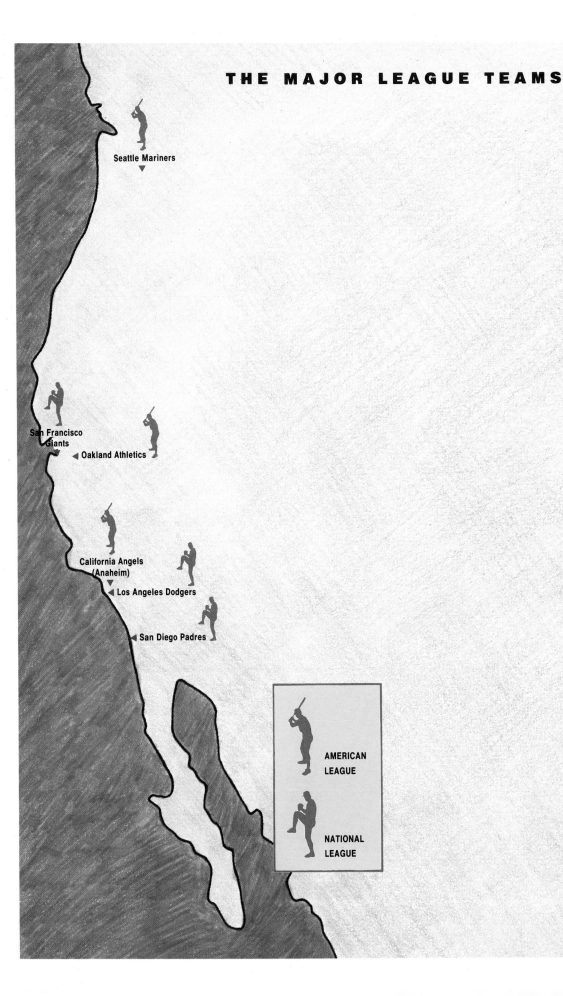

Seattle Mariners

San Francisco Giants

◀ Oakland Athletics

California Angels
(Anaheim)

◀ Los Angeles Dodgers

◀ San Diego Padres

AMERICAN
LEAGUE

NATIONAL
LEAGUE

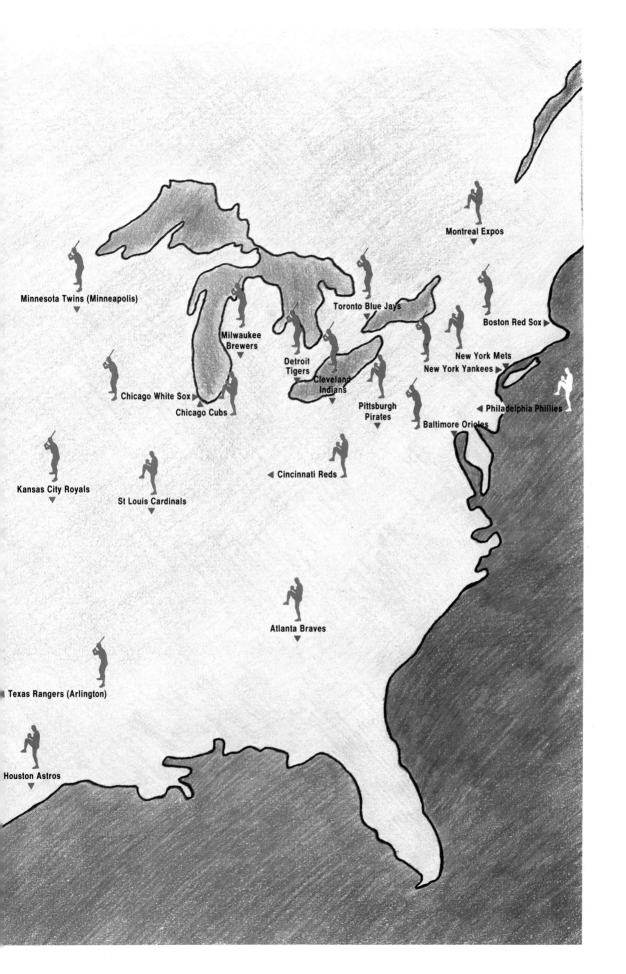

The 'Fall Classic' is played with great intensity over a ten-day period each October. The champions of the American League play the champions of the National League in a best-of-seven series which oscillates between the two cities in a highly publicised duel.

The first two games are played at the home of one club, then there is a day's travel. The next three games are played at the home of the other club, then there is another travel day. The final two games are played back at the first club. The National League and the American League champions alternate in having the first games.

In 1986 the first two games were held at the home of the National League's New York Mets, so in 1987 the American League champions will get two home games first. The fifth, sixth and/or seventh games in the World Series are not played if one team cannot be caught. Thus some World Series are won after only four games.

The World Series is played in late October, and because of the demands of network television, the games are all played at night to maximise the armchair audience. Games are usually played Saturday, Sunday, Tuesday, Wednesday, Thursday, Saturday, Sunday. By making the travel days on Monday and Friday the network gets four peak-time weekend transmissions for their investment in the event. Under the current contracts, ABC and NBC alternate World Series coverage. The network which does not have the World Series in any given year gets to cover both Leagues' Championship Series.

There is, in addition, an All-Star game, when two teams made up of the best players selected from each league, play each other.

FAR LEFT: The Boston Red Sox' Rich Gedman during the 1986 World Series.

LEFT: Baseball fans love team mascots and souvenirs.

BELOW: Boston's Huntington Avenue grounds, scene of the first World Series match in 1903.

LEAGUE CHAMPIONS & WORLD SERIES WINNERS

YEAR	A L CHAMPION	N L CHAMPION	WORLD SERIES WINNER
1903	Boston Red Sox	Pittsburgh Pirates	Boston, 5-3
1904	no World Series		
1905	Philadelphia Athletics	New York Giants	New York, 4-1
1906	Chicago White Sox	Chicago Cubs	Chicago (AL), 4-2
1907	Detroit Tigers	Chicago Cubs	Chicago, 4-0; 1 tie
1908	Detroit Tigers	Chicago Cubs	Chicago, 4-1
1909	Detroit Tigers	Pittsburgh Pirates	Pittsburgh, 4-3
1910	Philadelphia Athletics	Chicago Cubs	Philadelphia, 4-1
1911	Philadelphia Athletics	New York Giants	Philadelphia, 4-2
1912	Boston Red Sox	New York Giants	Boston, 4-3; 1 tie
1913	Philadelphia Athletics	New York Giants	Philadelphia, 4-1
1914	Philadelphia Athletics	Boston Braves	Boston, 4-0
1915	Boston Red Sox	Philadelphia Phillies	Boston, 4-1
1916	Boston Red Sox	Brooklyn Dodgers	Boston, 4-1
1917	Chicago White Sox	New York Giants	Chicago, 4-2
1918	Boston Red Sox	Chicago Cubs	Boston, 4-2
1919	Chicago White Sox	Cincinnati Reds	Cincinnati, 5-3
1920	Cleveland Indians	Brooklyn Dodgers	Cleveland, 5-2
1921	New York Yankees	New York Giants	New York (NL), 5-3
1922	New York Yankees	New York Giants	New York (NL), 4-0; 1 tie
1923	New York Yankees	New York Giants	New York (AL), 4-2
1924	Washington Senators	New York Giants	Washington, 4-3
1925	Washington Senators	Pittsburgh Pirates	Pittsburgh, 4-3
1926	New York Yankees	St Louis Cardinals	St Louis, 4-3
1927	New York Yankees	Pittsburgh Pirates	New York, 4-0
1928	New York Yankees	St Louis Cardinals	New York, 4-0
1929	Philadelphia Athletics	Chicago Cubs	Philadelphia, 4-1
1930	Philadelphia Athletics	St Louis Cardinals	Philadelphia, 4-2
1931	Philadelphia Athletics	St Louis Cardinals	St Louis, 4-3
1932	New York Yankees	Chicago Cubs	New York, 4-0
1933	Washington Senators	New York Giants	New York, 4-1
1934	Detroit Tigers	St Louis Cardinals	St Louis, 4-3
1935	Detroit Tigers	Chicago Cubs	Detroit, 4-2
1936	New York Yankees	New York Giants	New York (AL), 4-2
1937	New York Yankees	New York Giants	New York (AL), 4-1
1938	New York Yankees	Chicago Cubs	New York, 4-0
1939	New York Yankees	Cincinnati Reds	New York, 4-0
1940	Detroit Tigers	Cincinnati Reds	Cincinnati, 4-3
1941	New York Yankees	Brooklyn Dodgers	New York, 4-1
1942	New York Yankees	St Louis Cardinals	St Louis, 4-1

1943	New York Yankees	St Louis Cardinals	New York, 4-1
1944	St Louis Browns	St Louis Cardinals	St Louis (NL), 4-2
1945	Detroit Tigers	Chicago Cubs	Detroit, 4-3
1946	Boston Red Sox	St Louis Cardinals	St Louis, 4-3
1947	New York Yankees	Brooklyn Dodgers	New York, 4-3
1948	Cleveland Indians	Boston Braves	Cleveland, 4-2
1949	New York Yankees	Brooklyn Dodgers	New York, 4-1
1950	New York Yankees	Philadelphia Phillies	New York, 4-0
1951	New York Yankees	New York Giants	New York (AL), 4-2
1952	New York Yankees	Brooklyn Dodgers	New York, 4-3
1953	New York Yankees	Brooklyn Dodgers	New York, 4-2
1954	Cleveland Indians	New York Giants	New York, 4-0
1955	New York Yankees	Brooklyn Dodgers	Brooklyn, 4-3
1956	New York Yankees	Brooklyn Dodgers	New York, 4-3
1957	New York Yankees	Milwaukee Braves	Milwaukee, 4-3
1958	New York Yankees	Milwaukee Braves	New York, 4-3
1959	Chicago White Sox	Los Angeles Dodgers	Los Angeles, 4-2
1960	New York Yankees	Pittsburgh Pirates	Pittsburgh, 4-3
1961	New York Yankees	Cincinnati Reds	New York, 4-1
1962	New York Yankees	San Francisco Giants	New York, 4-3
1963	New York Yankees	Los Angeles Dodgers	Los Angeles, 4-0
1964	New York Yankees	St Louis Cardinals	St Louis, 4-3
1965	Minnesota Twins	Los Angeles Dodgers	Los Angeles, 4-3
1966	Baltimore Orioles	Los Angeles Dodgers	Baltimore, 4-0
1967	Boston Red Sox	St Louis Cardinals	St Louis, 4-3
1968	Detroit Tigers	St Louis Cardinals	Detroit, 4-3
1969	Baltimore Orioles	New York Mets	New York, 4-1
1970	Baltimore Orioles	Cincinnati Reds	Baltimore, 4-1
1971	Baltimore Orioles	Pittsburgh Pirates	Pittsburgh, 4-3
1972	Oakland Athletics	Cincinnati Reds	Oakland, 4-3
1973	Oakland Athletics	New York Mets	Oakland, 4-3
1974	Oakland Athletics	Los Angeles Dodgers	Oakland, 4-1
1975	Boston Red Sox	Cincinnati Reds	Cincinnati, 4-3
1976	New York Yankees	Cincinnati Reds	Cincinnati, 4-0
1977	New York Yankees	Los Angeles Dodgers	New York, 4-2
1978	New York Yankees	Los Angeles Dodgers	New York, 4-2
1979	Baltimore Orioles	Pittsburgh Pirates	Pittsburgh, 4-3
1980	Kansas City Royals	Philadelphia Phillies	Philadelphia, 4-2
1981	New York Yankees	Los Angeles Dodgers	Los Angeles, 4-2
1982	Milwaukee Brewers	St Louis Cardinals	St Louis, 4-3
1983	Baltimore Orioles	Philadelphia Phillies	Baltimore, 4-1
1984	Detroit Tigers	San Diego Padres	Detroit, 4-1
1985	Kansas City Royals	St Louis Cardinals	Kansas, 4-3
1986	Boston Red Sox	New York Mets	New York, 4-3

BOSTON		AB	R	H	RBI
Boggs	3B	5	2	3	0
Barrett	2B	4	1	3	2
Buckner	1B	5	0	0	0
Rice	LF	5	0	0	0
Evans	RF	4	0	1	2
Gedman	C	5	0	1	0
Hndrsn	CF	5	1	2	1
Owen	SS	4	1	3	0
Clemens	P	3	0	0	0
Greenwll	ph	1	0	0	0
Schiraldi	P	1	0	0	0
Stanley	P	0	0	0	0
TOTALS		42	5	13	5

NEW YORK		AB	R	H	RBI
Dykstra	CF	4	0	0	0
Backman	2B	4	0	1	0
Hernandez	1B	4	0	1	0
Carter	C	4	1	1	1
S'berry	RF	2	1	0	0
Knight	3B	4	2	2	2
Wilson	LF	5	0	1	0
Santana	SS	1	0	0	0
Ojeda	P	2	0	0	0
Heep	ph	1	0	0	0
Elster	ph	1	0	0	0
McDowell	P	0	0	0	0
Orosco	P	0	0	0	0
Aguilera	P	1	1	1	0
Mazzilli	ph	2	1	1	0
Johnson	ph	1	0	0	0
TOTALS		36	6	8	3

BOSTON	110	000	100	2	5
NEW YORK	000	020	010	3	6

BOSTON PITCHING	IP	H	R	ER	BB	SO	HBP	WP	PB	BALK
Clemens	7	4	2	1	2	8	0	0	0	0
Schiraldi (L)	2.2	4	4	3	2	1	0	0	0	0
Stanley	0	0	0	0	0	0	0	1	0	0

NEW YORK PITCHING	IP	H	R	ER	BB	SO	HBP	WP	PB	BALK
Ojeda	6	8	2	2	3	3	0	0	0	0
McDowell	1.2	2	1	0	3	1	0	0	0	0
Orosco	.1	0	0	0	0	0	0	0	0	0
Aguilera (W)	2	3	2	2	0	3	0	0	0	0

E	none	**LOB** : NY 8, BOS 14		
2B	**BOS** :	Evans, Boggs.	**NY** : none	
3B	**BOS** :	none	**NY** : none	
HR	**BOS** :	Henderson	**NY** : none	

Time : 4.02   **Attendance** : 55,078

HOW TO READ A BOXSCORE

This is the boxscore which appeared in the American newspapers after the famous Game 6 in the 1986 World Series. It's not as complicated as it looks at first glance, and the key will help you make head and tail of it.

─────── KEY ───────

In the line above the batting scores:
AB = at bats, **R** = runs, **H** = hits, **RBI** = runs batted in.

The figures for the fourth batter in each line-up mean:
For **Rice, LF** means he is the **Boston Red Sox left field**, and he came into bat five times, but scored no runs, hits or runs batted in.
For **Carter, C** means he is the **New York Mets catcher**, the figures that he came into bat four times, scored one run, one hit and one run batted in.
CF means **center field**, **R** means **right field**, **SS** short stop, **P** pitcher, and **1B**, **2B** and **3B** mean **first base, second base** and **third base**.
The **ph** for various batters means they are **pinch hitters**.

The two lines for **Boston** and **New York** show the runs scored in each inning, the nine innings being grouped in threes, and the extra inning necessary being separate, followed by the final total of runs (6-5 to New York).

The abbreviations at the top of the pitching columns mean:
IP = innings pitched, **H** = hits, **R** = runs, **ER** = earned runs, **BB** = bases on balls, **SO** = strike-outs, **HBP** = hit by pitch, **WP** = wild pitch (in this game, Stanley's helped New York to win), **PB** = passed balls.

In the details at the foot of the boxscore:
E = errors, **LOB** = batters left on base, **2B** = two-base hits (achieved by Evans and Boggs), **3B** = three-base hits, **HR** = home runs (achieved by Henderson).
The game lasted four hours and two minutes.

BASEBALL & AMERICAN ★ CULTURE ★

Baseball has made a great impact on American culture and language. Some of the vocabulary of the sport has become not only a part of the language in America, but has enriched our own imagery as well. You might have 'made a pitch' for something, or 'struck out' when looking for something; some of your more original ideas may have come out of 'left field'. You might have 'touched base' with a business colleague, or discussed 'ballpark figures' with him. You might even have 'made a play' for something (or someone!) and found you were in a 'different ballgame'.

Advertisers in America have regularly used baseball to sell their products: perhaps the most famous slogan in American advertising was coined by General Motors, and could almost be used to sell America itself – 'Baseball, hot-dogs, apple pie and Chevrolet.'

ABOVE: Baseball is an integral part of life from early childhood for every true-blooded American.

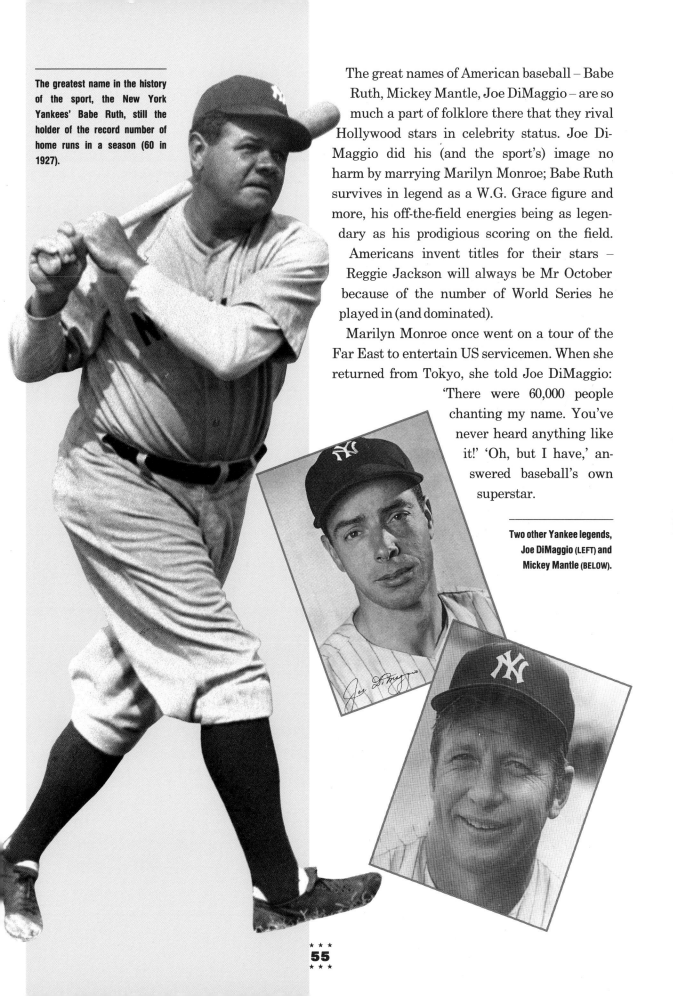

The great names of American baseball – Babe Ruth, Mickey Mantle, Joe DiMaggio – are so much a part of folklore there that they rival Hollywood stars in celebrity status. Joe DiMaggio did his (and the sport's) image no harm by marrying Marilyn Monroe; Babe Ruth survives in legend as a W.G. Grace figure and more, his off-the-field energies being as legendary as his prodigious scoring on the field.

Americans invent titles for their stars – Reggie Jackson will always be Mr October because of the number of World Series he played in (and dominated).

Marilyn Monroe once went on a tour of the Far East to entertain US servicemen. When she returned from Tokyo, she told Joe DiMaggio: 'There were 60,000 people chanting my name. You've never heard anything like it!' 'Oh, but I have,' answered baseball's own superstar.

Two other Yankee legends, Joe DiMaggio (LEFT) and Mickey Mantle (BELOW).

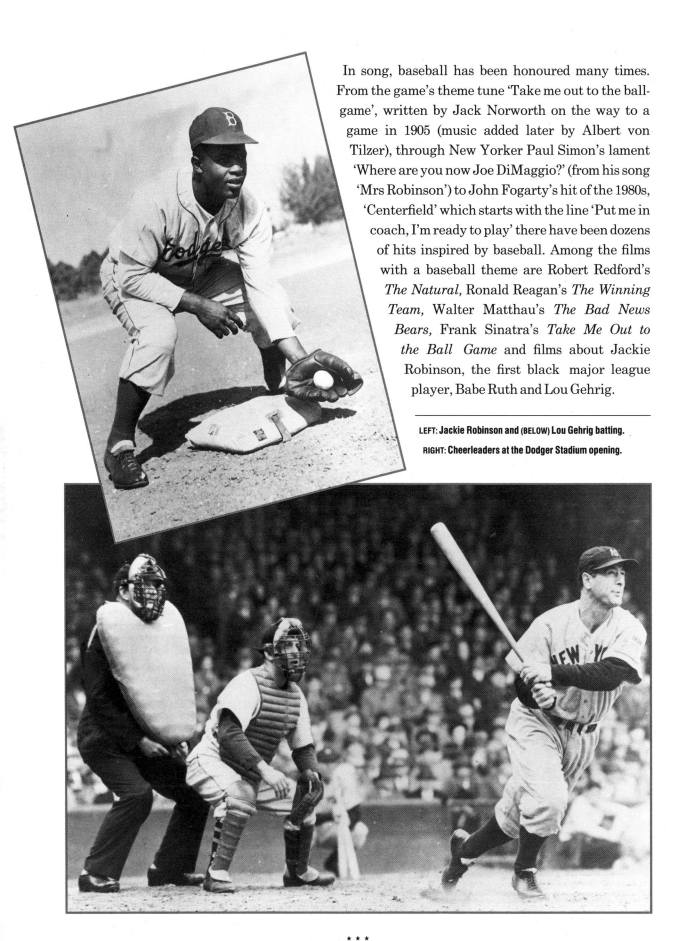

In song, baseball has been honoured many times. From the game's theme tune 'Take me out to the ball-game', written by Jack Norworth on the way to a game in 1905 (music added later by Albert von Tilzer), through New Yorker Paul Simon's lament 'Where are you now Joe DiMaggio?' (from his song 'Mrs Robinson') to John Fogarty's hit of the 1980s, 'Centerfield' which starts with the line 'Put me in coach, I'm ready to play' there have been dozens of hits inspired by baseball. Among the films with a baseball theme are Robert Redford's *The Natural,* Ronald Reagan's *The Winning Team,* Walter Matthau's *The Bad News Bears,* Frank Sinatra's *Take Me Out to the Ball Game* and films about Jackie Robinson, the first black major league player, Babe Ruth and Lou Gehrig.

LEFT: **Jackie Robinson and (BELOW) Lou Gehrig batting.**
RIGHT: **Cheerleaders at the Dodger Stadium opening.**

LEFT: Liz Taylor.

LEFT: The late
Danny Kaye.

ABOVE: Bob Boone.

Baseball has done much to popularise that great American invention the hot-dog, and perhaps *vice versa*. The most famous hot-dog in all of American sports is available at Dodger Stadium in Los Angeles. The Dodger Dog is as much a part of baseball as the Seventh Inning Stretch, where all fans stand up to stretch their legs usually to the accompaniment of 'Take me out to the ballgame'. The second most famous refreshment is Boston's Fenway Frank.

'What made Milwaukee famous made a loser out of me' – at County Stadium, Milwaukee, four different kinds of beer are on sale. What else would you expect from a brewing town? And guess which beer is available at Busch Stadium in St Louis, where the ballclub is owned by the Busch family, part of Anheiser-Busch, the brewers of Budweiser.

The American writer George Plimpton has a theory that the smaller the ball involved in a sport, the better the quality of the writing about it. He reckons that there are virtually no good books written about basketball, few about American football, some good ones on baseball and lots on golf. British readers will appreciate both the literary and sporting qualities of books by the *Washington Post* baseball writer Thomas Bosworth.

Baseball is now covered on a ball-by-ball basis on both radio and television. The first World Series on radio was the 1921 New York 'derby' between the Giants and the Yankees. The Chicago Cubs were first with regular coverage in 1924. Ronald Reagan was a baseball radio announcer in Chicago before the war – the last war – before his later career as a *Spitting Image* puppet.

The first televised game came from NBC in 1939 from the Brooklyn Stadium of the Dodgers, who were playing the Reds.

ABOVE RIGHT: **The famous Dodger Dog . . .**

. . . and if you don't fancy one of them, how about peanuts? (FAR RIGHT).

BASEBALL LORE

There could be, and probably is, a book this size of the wise and funny things baseball folk have said over the years. Here are just four quotations which do a lot, I think, to sum up the importance of the game in American life:

'Whoever would understand the heart and mind of America had better learn baseball.'
writer/historian **Jacques Barzun**

'Next to religion, baseball has had a greater impact on the American people than any other institution.'
former President **Herbert Hoover**

'Say this much for Major League baseball, it is beyond any question the greatest conversation piece invented in America.'
writer/historian **Bruce Catton**

'You spend a good piece of your life gripping a baseball, and in the end it turns out that it was the other way around all the time.'
former pitcher **Jim Bouton**

BASEBALL & AMERICAN TV

There is no great tradition of away support in American sport, primarily because of the great distances between cities. For this reason every team's away games are normally televised live in their home cities. In the NFL, for example, it is a major part of the contracts NBC and CBS hold for Sunday afternoon coverage of American football that they screen every game in the home city of the away team.

In professional basketball and in baseball the teams usually put together a television deal in their own cities that enables fans to see all road games live and in full.

Home games are a different matter. Clubs want to attract a large paying gate and games are not shown locally on live 'free' television. There has been a growth recently in local 'pay-tv' operations which allow subscribers to watch home games from the comfort of their own armchairs. Some of the clubs, for example the Los Angeles Dodgers, are major partners in cable enterprises in their cities.

Some teams, however, have their home games shown across the USA on the so-called 'super-stations'. The best example of this is the Atlanta Braves, whose games are shown nationally on cable stations by WTBS. It is of course no coincidence that both the Braves and WTBS are owned by Ted Turner. He bought the Braves to provide instant programming for his station, programming that filled a lot of hours relatively inexpensively and was attractive to viewers and advertisers alike. All he needs is for the Braves to have a winning team!

On a national level too are the networks, led by NBC, who are recognised as the best at covering baseball. NBC's *Game of the Week* is a national institution, covering a live game every Saturday afternoon. The doyen of baseball announcers, Vin Scully, has a national audience, after spending a lifetime as the voice of the Dodgers in both Los Angeles and Brooklyn.

ABC covers baseball on Monday nights in the latter part of the season, in a companion series to *Monday Night Football*. The two networks alternate with their coverage of the World Series, the play-offs and the annual All-Star Game.

Interestingly, both networks lose substantial amounts of money on their current baseball contracts and it is likely that there will be big changes when negotiations start for the 1990 season.

Harry Coyne has directed baseball for NBC for over 30 years and has seen the coverage of the sport improve as technology has improved, from perhaps three cameras shooting in black and white with no replays and no graphics to the eleven cameras and nine tape machines he had at his disposal for the 1986 World Series. After colour and slow motion, the biggest change in television coverage of baseball came 25 years ago when lenses became good enough to site a camera out at center field. This camera gives the alternative 'master shot', looking past the pitcher towards the batter. The huge close-ups of the batter are taken from cameras in the dug-outs, and the close-up of the pitcher, often pulling back with the pitch, are taken from a camera behind the catcher which peeks through a hole in the backstop.

Channel 4 gets its pictures from NBC or ABC, although it usually has its own crew at the game to supply its own material, too. The other part of what has been a very successful partnership is Major League Baseball Productions which receives tapes of every game played, makes all kinds of highlight shows and contributes a number of the amusing and entertaining music sequences which are sprinkled throughout Channel 4 programmes.

Spectators tend to form a mass of the home team's colours, like these Dodgers fans. Away spectators support from the comfort of their armchairs.

BASEBALL &
CHANNEL 4

★ ★ ★ ★ ★ ★

American football had been running on Channel 4 for only a few weeks when letters began arriving saying: 'This is great, why don't you try baseball?' The trickle became a flood and by the end of 1985 it was obvious that baseball must be given a shot – but in what form? It was eventually decided to try an unusual idea for British television, but not unusual in America: the doubleheader. On New Year's morning 1986, Channel 4 opened with 90 minutes of American football play-off action, followed by 90 minutes of

World Series baseball, and surprisingly more people watched the baseball than the football. More importantly, many more letters were received asking to see more of America's favourite pastime.

For British audiences, the first priority was to foster an understanding of the fundamentals of the sport, which seemed best achieved by showing highlights of the not-so-key games in

BELOW AND RIGHT: The first World Series to be shown extensively on British TV was also one of the most exciting.

quick order, followed by a long look at the best game available. This is because the natural rhythm and pace of the game can be appreciated only if the viewer sees the balls and strikes as well as the hits, and the apparently unexciting events like a player intentionally walked. In other words, to get the flavour, the viewer must see the game's 'lowlights' as well as the highlights. To cut baseball too tight would make the game much more difficult to understand and enjoy, in the way that a succession of boundaries and wickets would not lead to a full understanding of cricket.

Those successful 90 minutes on New Year's Day 1986 were followed by 10 hours of coverage of the 1986 play-offs and World Series the following October. Further coverage for 1987 was then planned, and if audiences continue to grow then a game of the week, at least in the second half of the season, will surely follow.

THE TEAMS
★ ★   ★ ★

★ ★ ★ ★ ★ ★ ★

Baseball's twenty-six major league teams are as different as chalk and, well, Philadelphia cream cheese. Each team starts the season with a roster of players (given here at the end of each entry) but with a transfer market as active as British football's, who knows who will be playing on the winning side at the end of the World Series?

The Toronto Blue Jays (MAIN PICTURE), St Louis Cardinals v. New York Mets (LEFT), and the California Angels v. Oakland Athletics (ABOVE).

ATLANTA BRAVES

The Braves came to the sprawling southern city of Atlanta from Boston by way of Milwaukee. They had been World Champions in both of their previous home cities, but success seems to have gone with the wind once the Braves arrived in Atlanta.

The Boston Braves had frequent success in the first third of this century, even coming from last place to first in the National League in 1914. The 'Miracle Braves' went on to win the World Series. The legendary Babe Ruth, the W.G. Grace of baseball, finished his career with the Braves, having begun it in the same city with the Red Sox.

Milwaukee became the home of the Braves in the land of the free in 1953, the first move of a NL club in modern times. Milwaukee had never had a professional sports franchise, and once the novelty of limited success had worn off the city just wasn't large enough to support the club. They won and lost World Series in the late 1950s, but lack of further success forced another move, the first time a club had moved itself twice.

The Atlanta-Fulton County Stadium was built on the promise of a move by the Braves to the city, and was opened for the start of the 1966 season. The stadium, a modern circular design known in the game as being of the cookie-cutter variety, lies between the airport and the city and later became home to the Atlanta Falcons NFL team.

Owned by the millionaire yachtsman and television entrepreneur Ted Turner, the Braves are seen throughout the USA almost every night on Turner's self-styled superstation WTBS. The Atlanta Braves are, with typical Turner modesty, known by the broadcasters as 'America's Team'.

Atlanta, put to the torch in 1864 by distinctly unsporting Yankees, is now a fast-growing city in that part of America known, not just for weather reasons, as the Sun Belt. Light industry is attracted to the region, and a young upwardly mobile population of workers follows it from the older, heavier industries of the north and northeast. It all sounds ideal territory in which to transplant a baseball team, but sadly the Braves have only two successes to boast about during their time in Atlanta – winning the National League's western division in 1969 and 1982, although on neither occasion did they reach the World Series. In 1982, they set a major league record by winning their first 13 games – a record that was equalled in 1987 by the Milwaukee Brewers.

Atlanta's stadium is on the small side, so recent Braves teams have tried to capitalise on this by building power hitting teams. Their most famous hitter was Henry Aaron who, on 8 April 1974, beat Babe Ruth's lifetime record of 714 home runs by hitting a pitch to the far left of Fulton County Stadium. He went on to notch up a career 755 home runs. Dale Murphy has been a more recent Braves slugger, while pitcher Bob Horner is now a big star with the Yakult Swallows in Japan.

Atlanta needs a successful baseball team, and Ted Turner needs the Braves' success to generate bigger crowds and greater television revenues to justify his investment in the team. Without success there is a very real chance that the people of Atlanta, frankly, won't give a damn about their team.

ATLANTA-FULTON COUNTY STADIUM

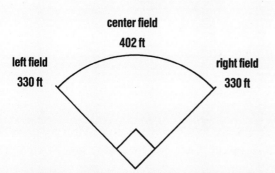

center field
402 ft

left field
330 ft

right field
330 ft

Record-breaking Brave Henry Aaron
and team owner, Ted Turner (INSET).

ATLANTA BRAVES

PO Box 4064
Atlanta, Georgia 30302
Tel: (404) 522 7630

Stadium: Atlanta-Fulton
County Stadium

Opened: 12 April 1966

Capacity: 52,006

Surface: Grass

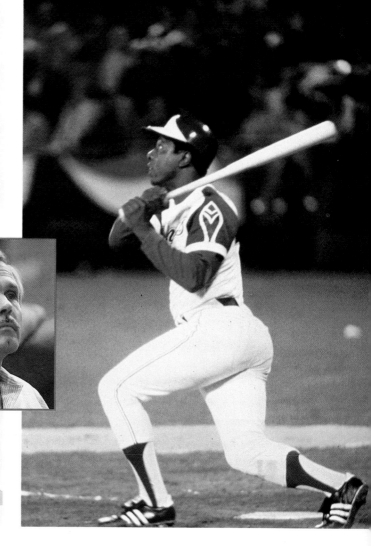

World Series: None

Pitchers: Jim Acker (r), Doyle Alexander (l), Paul Assenmacher (l), Jeff Dedmon (r), Gene Garber (r), Rick Mahler (r), Ed Olwine (l), Randy O'Neal (r), David Palmer (r), Charlie Puleo (r), Zane Smith (l)

Catchers: Bruce Benedict, Ted Simmons, Ozzie Virgil

Infielders: Glenn Hubbard, Craig Nettles, Ken Oberkfell, Gerald Perry, Rafael Ramirez, Andres Thomas

Outfielders: Ken Griffey, Albert Hall, Dion James, Dale Murphy, Gary Roenicke

Manager: Chuck Tanner

BALTIMORE ORIOLES

American League

★ ★ ★ ★ ★

This is one of the great clubs in American baseball, although the city is unexciting and much of the area has gone through hard times. To many travellers through the years Baltimore has been just a station on the Washington–New York railway, but the city is a seaport on the north end of Chesapeake Bay and it is beginning to enjoy an economic resurgence, as the city slowly spreads out until it meets the outer edges of the national capital.

As Maryland's only baseball team, it would be nice to report that the Orioles play in a cookie-cutter stadium, but in fact they play in a traditional 1949-built home just about close enough to Washington to attract baseball-starved day trippers from DC. The horseshoe-shaped stadium allows the crowd to watch from close quarters. The Baltimore Colts football team shared the stadium until their move to Indianapolis after the 1983 season, and the damage the Colts did to the natural grass sometimes made late-season baseball interesting for the fielding team in Orioles' games.

The Orioles started their life in Milwaukee in 1901, but only lasted a year there before becoming the St Louis Browns. The move to Baltimore came about in 1954, the first American League club to move in modern times. The then owner of the club wanted to move out west to Los Angeles but the other owners would not agree. They could not, however, stop the owner selling the club to Bill Veeck, a brewery owner, who set up shop in Baltimore.

Bill Veeck sometimes treated America's favourite pastime with scant respect, having at various times fielded a midget batter (think what that does to the strike zone!), a one-armed fielder, and the immortal Satchel Paige ('Never look back, someone may be gaining on you!').

The big names in Orioles' history were Jim Palmer, a great pitcher who achieved equal fame by posing in his underpants for advertisements, and his manager Earl Weaver. Weaver joined the Orioles in 1969, three years after the club had won their first World Series. In the next ten years, the Orioles achieved a stunning run of success – reaching the World Series in 1969 (lost), 1970 (won), 1971 (lost) and 1979 (lost). The Orioles won the 1983 World Series under Weaver's successor, Jo Altobelli.

Palmer, a three-times Pitcher of the Year, was a player of great intelligence, who is now bringing insight into the ABC TV commentary booth. The brains behind the ballclub now come from an unusual father/son combination. Cal Ripken Sr is the manager, and his son, Jr, runs the team from first base.

Frank Robinson, the first black manager in baseball with Cleveland, starred for the Orioles in the last generation of ballplayers, along with another Robinson, Brooks, who some say was the finest third baseman there has ever been.

If you ever visit the Orioles be sure to have some crab cakes with your beer (baseball is full of culinary surprises!) and admire the flag which flies over the stadium. This version of the Stars and Stripes has 15 stars and is a replica of the one that flew over nearby Fort McHenry in Baltimore Harbour. The fort saw explosive action in the War of 1812, although why the Orioles commemorate this is long forgotten.

Oriole manager Cal Ripkin Sr (ABOVE RIGHT) and his son, infielder Cal Jr (FAR RIGHT).

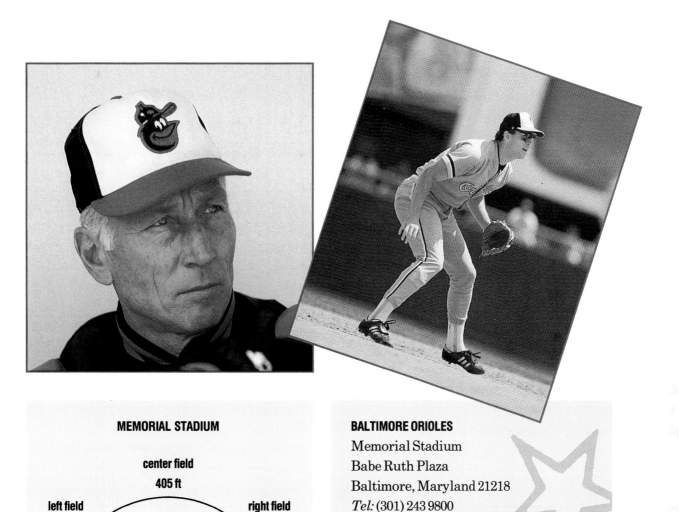

MEMORIAL STADIUM

center field
405 ft

left field
309 ft

right field
309 ft

BALTIMORE ORIOLES
Memorial Stadium
Babe Ruth Plaza
Baltimore, Maryland 21218
Tel: (301) 243 9800

Stadium: Memorial Stadium

Opened: 1949, saw its first American
League game on 15 April 1954

Capacity: 54,076 **Surface:** Grass

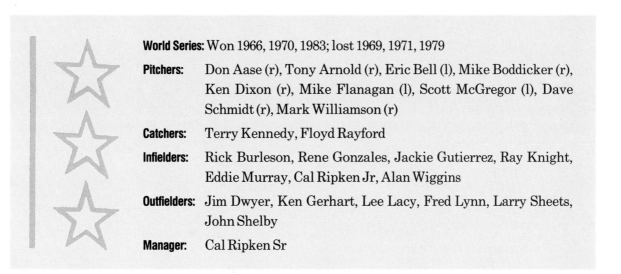

World Series: Won 1966, 1970, 1983; lost 1969, 1971, 1979

Pitchers: Don Aase (r), Tony Arnold (r), Eric Bell (l), Mike Boddicker (r), Ken Dixon (r), Mike Flanagan (l), Scott McGregor (l), Dave Schmidt (r), Mark Williamson (r)

Catchers: Terry Kennedy, Floyd Rayford

Infielders: Rick Burleson, Rene Gonzales, Jackie Gutierrez, Ray Knight, Eddie Murray, Cal Ripken Jr, Alan Wiggins

Outfielders: Jim Dwyer, Ken Gerhart, Lee Lacy, Fred Lynn, Larry Sheets, John Shelby

Manager: Cal Ripken Sr

★ ★ ★ ★ ★

The Boston Red Sox – the team of ultimate frustration. Without a World Series win since the First World War – and with a variety of unlucky and inept near-misses since – the baseball fans of Beantown are a long-suffering lot.

Boston provides an easy introduction to America for visitors from Britain because New England is a lot more like the old one than the rest of the USA. Boston is an attractive city with its Back Bay lined with fine examples of eighteenth- and nineteenth-century architecture built by the shipping magnates who had dominated the commerce of the city since before the Boston Tea Party. There is plenty of open space too, like Boston Common where you can be charmed by squirrels eating out of your hand. And the natives know that 'tomatoes' is pronounced 'tomahtoes' and not 'tomaytoes'.

In baseball terms too, Boston counts as 'traditional' – boasting real grass and one of the architectural wonders of the sport, Fenway Park itself. This corner of New England that shall remain forever home to the Boston Red Sox was built for the 1912 season, and was opened on the day the *Titanic* went down. Fenway Park remains a quaint anachronism in a sport that is now full of Astroturf, Diamond Vision and electronic hype. The stadium is largely unaltered from the 1930s – wooden seats, green paint and a manual scoreboard that is a close relative to some of the older cricket scoreboards still in use in Britain.

Fenway Park is dominated by the Green Monster, not a character from *Sesame Street*, but a 37-foot high wall which dominates left field and the nightmares of pitchers and hitters alike. It is huge – easily the most dominating characteristic of any ballpark in the major leagues. From a batting point of view the Green Monster is both good news and bad news. The bad news is that if you try and hit a home run over it you probably won't. The ball will almost certainly rebound off it, turning your home run into at best a double. The good news, however, is that the wall is only 315 feet away from the batter and some of the fly balls that would get caught in the outfield in other parks will sail over the wall here for unexpected home runs. By and large, pitchers distrust the Monster too, particularly left-handers who can be taken on by ambitious right-handed hitters who sometimes 'pull' the ball high enough to clear the wall and to land it in Landsdowne Street behind. The Green Monster is as tall as a three-storey house and is one of the most unforgettable sights in baseball.

Patrolling the Green Monster has proved to be a specialist job, and some of the Red Sox left-fielders have become legendary. Duffy Lewis made the position his own through the 1920s, and only three men have played there with any regularity since the last war – Ted Williams, the first $100,000 a year baseball player, Carl Yastrgemski, and the current choice Jim Rice. Williams was the last man to bat .400 (in 1941) and has the distinction, probably unique, of hitting a home run in his last at bat before retirement.

Boston, long a leading American centre of commerce and sports, for a time supported two major league baseball clubs. The first to open up

Carl Yastrgemski, renowned Red Sox left-infielder.

there were the Boston Braves who played in the National League until moving to Milwaukee in 1952 and then finally to Atlanta.

The Red Sox have sported, or suffered, a variety of owners. One of the earliest, Harry Frazeer, took the unlikely and unpopular decision to trade the biggest name baseball has ever known by selling Babe Ruth to the New York Yankees in 1920. Ruth in those days played as both a pitcher and an outfielder (but not at the same time!) and although the trade was early in his career he was even then the sport's number one attraction. Frazeer was a showbiz impressario in New York and his reason for selling Ruth to Boston's great rivals the Yankees was to set up a production of 'No No Nanette' on Broadway. The $50,000 Frazeer received for Ruth kept the show going but didn't do much for the baseball team!

To the end of the Second World War, when baseball was predominantly a North Eastern sport, the American League was made up of clubs that couldn't get a franchise in the older and more established National League. In the days before air travel, when teams moved around by rail, there were longer gaps between games, and with no team west of St Louis or south of Washington, the frequently broadcast teams of Boston, Detroit and New York were the class acts in major league baseball. Each club had not only a local and regional following but a national one too. In Boston's case it remained a frustrated following.

The Bo Sox have not won a World Series since 1918. In 1946, when baseball became a sport of truly national interest and importance, they lost to St Louis largely through mistakes of their own making. They lost to the Cardinals again in 1967 and in 1975 to a Pete Rose-inspired Cincinnati Reds. And then in 1986, in the first World Series to be given extensive coverage on Britain's Channel 4, they lost to the New York Mets after being two games up and then just one pitch away from a 4 games to 2 Series victory. It seemed somehow par for the course to see the ball pass through Bill Buckner's aching legs, and for the Sox to lose a game and then the Series to a team which scores high on arrogance but low on tradition.

The Boston club has been, over the years, one for sluggers. The Red Sox have tended to prefer to hit their way to a winning season rather than finesse their way there with subtle pitching. However, the current line-up includes, in Roger Clemens, a pitcher of the very highest quality who in 1986 struck out a major league record of 20 batters in a memorable night game against the Seattle Mariners. On the other hand, they also have the flamboyant Dennis 'Oil Can' Boyd who could be described as the Hurricane Higgins of baseball. Wade Boggs leads the Red Sox batting line-up and has topped the American League averages in three of the last five seasons.

Although Democratic in its politics, Boston is not a city renowned for its liberal attitude to racial integration in sports. The Boston Celtics have won the world championship of professional basketball unusually with a predominantly white line-up, and it does the Red Sox no credit to have been the last major league baseball club to sign a black to its roster. It was as late as 1959 when Boston grudgingly signed the black Pumpsie Green who, it was said, was not even a good player. This was 22 years after the Brooklyn Dodgers signed the first black player of modern times – Jackie Robinson.

Finally, and only sports could come up with a 'would you believe it' like this, the Boston Red Sox don't play in red socks! What we British call socks are white and are what Americans have charmlessly christened 'sanitary hose'! The red bits up the side of the ankles are what have given Boston their nickname. Just think, they could have called themselves the Boston White Sanitary Hose!

FENWAY PARK

center field
390 ft

left field
315 ft

right field
302 ft

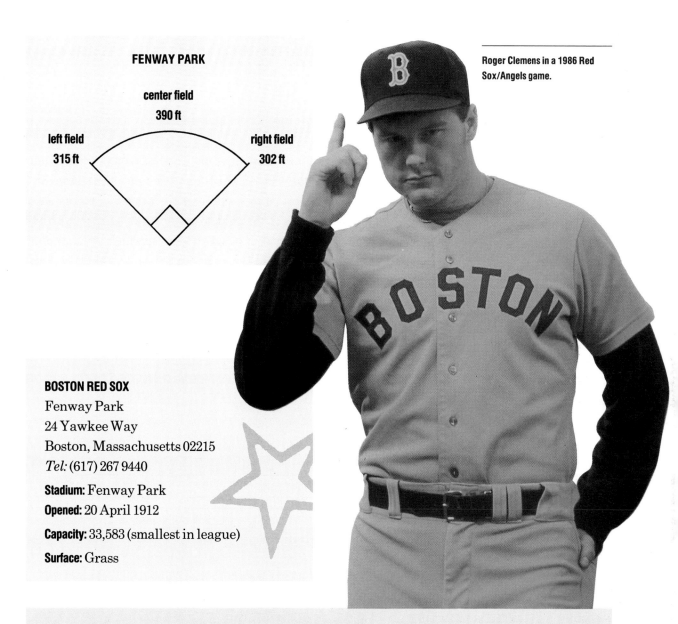

BOSTON RED SOX
Fenway Park
24 Yawkee Way
Boston, Massachusetts 02215
Tel: (617) 267 9440

Stadium: Fenway Park
Opened: 20 April 1912
Capacity: 33,583 (smallest in league)
Surface: Grass

World Series: Won 1903, 1912, 1915, 1916, 1918; lost 1946, 1967, 1975, 1986

Pitchers: Roger Clemens (r), Steve Crawford (r), Wes Gardner (r), Bruce Hurst (l), Al Nipper (r), Joe Sambito (l), Calvin Schiraldi (r), Jeff Sellers (r), Bob Stanley (r), Rob Woodward (r)

Catchers: Rich Gedman, Marc Sullivan, Danny Sheaffer, Dave Sax

Infielders: Marty Barrett, Wade Boggs, Bill Buckner, Pat Dodson, Spike Owen, Ed Romero

Outfielders: Don Baylor, Dwight Evans, Mike Greenwell, Dave Henderson, Jim Rice

Manager: John McNamara

CALIFORNIA ANGELS

A m e r i c a n L e a g u e

★ ★ ★ ★ ★ ★

It could only happen in California – a ballclub owned by a singing cowboy, playing its games at Disneyland in one of the biggest car parks in the world, and serving its fans with picnic areas and wine bars. Welcome to the Magic Kingdom!

There have been minor league Los Angeles Angels for generations, but the major league team of that name was born in 1961 with the first recent expansion of the American League. The story has it that Gene Autry, the singing cowboy of countless Hollywood films, went to an owners' meeting to try and buy broadcasting rights to a team for his radio station and came away owning a franchise.

The city hosted their first American League games in a small stadium called Wrigley Field (the LA Dodgers meanwhile being tenants at the Coliseum until opening their own stadium in Chavez Ravine in 1962). Eventually the two LA ballclubs shared the same stadium, although National League fans knew it as Dodger Stadium, and American League fans knew it as Chavez Ravine! The relationship was always uneasy, the *Sporting News* reporting that an Angels accountant objected to paying for 50 per cent of the toilet paper when 76 per cent of the customers were watching Dodgers' games!

Every Hollywood story needs its stars, and the Angels have always been hell-bent on assembling a team of big names, some of them decidedly in the twilight of their careers. Fred Lynn, Bobby Grich, Rod Carew and the biggest of them all, Reggie Jackson, have all been used to attract the blasé Californian to the ballpark.

The Angels did well to finish third in their second year, and have had three league championship sides, the last being in 1986 when they lost a thrilling Series to the Boston Red Sox. They have in Wally Joyner a young star, one of the best in the league, to go with their older superstars. Carew has now retired, and Jackson has gone north for yet another farewell appearance – this time with the Oakland Athletics. It all seems a long way since the Angels fielded Dick Stuart, a good home run hitter, but a man who enjoyed a reputation as the world's worst fielder – he was more likely to be hit by the ball than to catch it!

Anaheim, the urban part of Orange County indistinguishable from most of the Los Angeles sprawl, decided to help the Angels break free from their uneasy joint tenancy with the Dodgers, and in 1966 the Angels moved to Anaheim and became the California Angels.

The plan was to build a new stadium learning from other clubs' mistakes, using the good ideas and forgetting the bad. It is arguable whether they succeeded or not, but by the time Anaheim added the missing segment of a circular stadium, and an upper deck in order to accommodate football's Los Angeles Rams, there was no doubt that they had created an impressive if dull ballpark.

Living just over the road from Disneyland, the Angels have never been safe from the Mickey Mouse syndrome – but a strong 1986 has led the club to believe that 1987 could be their year. They have for instance refused a booking for another sport to use Anaheim Stadium in October 1987 on the grounds that they may be needing it for World Series games!

Angels owner Gene Autry (FAR RIGHT) with Rod Carew.

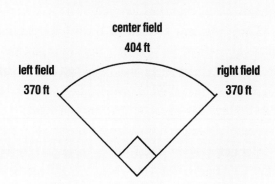

ANAHEIM STADIUM

center field
404 ft

left field
370 ft

right field
370 ft

CALIFORNIA ANGELS
PO Box 2000
Anaheim, California 92803
Tel: (714) 937 6700

Stadium: Anaheim Stadium
Opened: 1966
Capacity: 64,573
Surface: Grass

World Series: None

Pitchers: DeWayne Buice (r), John Candelaria (l), Ray Chadwick (r), Stew Cliburn (r), Mike Cook (r), Bill Fraser (r), Gary Lucas (l), Urbano Lugo (r), Kirk McCaskill (r), Donnie Moore (r), Don Sutton (r), Mike Witt (r)

Catchers: Darrell Miller, Jerry Narron, Butch Wynegar

Infielders: Doug DeCinces, Jack Howell, Wally Joyner, Mark McLemore, Gus Polidor, Dick Schofield

Outfielders: Brian Downing, George Hendrick, Ruppert Jones, Gary Pettis, Mark Ryal, Devon White

Manager: Gene Mauch

CHICAGO CUBS
National League

★ ★ ★ ★ ★ ★

They call Chicago the Windy City, and even in summer there is a wind which blows across Wrigley Field, usually from behind the pitchers' mound. Visiting pitchers come to the ground early to gaze up at the huge flag which flutters above the manual scoreboard. Ernie Banks, a colourful and successful Cubs fielder used to look at the flag and, if it blew in the right direction, would cheerfully suggest 'It's such a beautiful day, let's play two [games].' Once in a while however, the mitt would be on the other hand and the batters would be favoured. On one windy day in Chicago, the Phillies arrived to find the wind blowing from behind the plate and won the game 23-22.

The Cubs' home is to many people *the* great park – not just the oldest stadium in the National League, but one where you can almost peel the history off the ivy-clad walls. Late in the season the ivy covers the stadium's outfield wall to a depth of 18 inches, enough to cushion a collision with a fielder or to 'catch' a home run within its foliage (a base runner can advance two bases if the fielder cannot find the ball!). It's a very small park – small enough for fans in the bleachers to sit wearing hard hats – and the streets around Wrigley Field are regularly under home-run attack, the balls bouncing away down the sidewalks. You can watch games from the tops of neighbours' houses, or if you pay money for your seat you are close enough to hear the players talk, and they can hear every comment made from the stands.

Those same neighbours are the reason that Wrigley Field is the only park in the major leagues without lights, they having always objected to any plans to install floodlights there. Contrary to public belief, the club and its owners *do* want lights, and went so far as to have them delivered in the early 1940s, but the Wrigley family donated them to the Navy to light one of the Great Lakes dockyards so that it could work around the clock fuelling the war effort. Nowadays the installation of lights would need a state law to be repealed, but with the television networks demanding more and more night games it may only take the Cubs to reach a World Series for TV clout to change not only tradition but the law itself.

The Cubs are a team of traditions, having played in ten World Series – but their last time as World Champions was way back in 1908, and their last losing World Series was in 1945. However those Cubs fans remain loyal, probably the most loyal of them all.

The owners of the Cubs were the Wrigley family, famous for Chewleys Wriggling Gum of course, and their wonderful old stadium was at one time home to the National Football League's Chicago Bears – a home that had an illegal 8-yard touchdown zone at one end, incidentally, because the stadium is too small for the regulation 10 yards. The Club is now owned by the *Chicago Tribune* newspaper group.

It's true that since the last war the Cubs have done little right. Nobody's sure whether all those day games in the summer sun are the reason. And if they are the reason, whether the lack of success is because of long days in the sun or long nights on the town!

Wrigley Field, Chicago, home of the Cubs.

WRIGLEY FIELD

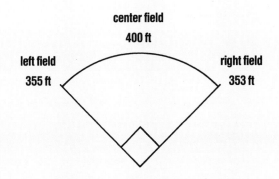

center field
400 ft

left field
355 ft

right field
353 ft

CHICAGO CUBS

Clark & Addison St
Chicago, Illinois 60613
Tel: (312) 281 5050

Stadium: Wrigley Field
Opened: 20 April 1916 (oldest in National League), the only major league stadium without lights
Capacity: 38,040
Surface: Grass

World Series: Won 1907, 1908; lost 1906, 1910, 1918, 1924, 1932, 1935, 1938, 1945

Pitchers: Ron Davis (r), Frank DiPino (l), Les Lancaster (r), Ed Lynch (r), Greg Maddux (r), Jamie Moyer (l), Dickie Noles (r), Lee Smith (r), Rick Sutcliffe (r), Steve Trout (l)

Catchers: Jody Davis, Jim Sundberg

Infielders: Shawon Dunston, Leon Durham, Keith Moreland, Ryne Sandberg, Manny Trillo

Outfielders: Andre Dawson, Brian Dayett, Bob Dernier, Dave Martinez, Gary Matthews, Jerry Mumphrey, Chico Walker

Manager: Gene Michael

CHICAGO WHITE SOX

American League

★ ★ ★ ★ ★ ★

Uniquely in baseball, but in common with jazz, Chicago is split right down the middle – people who live in the north of the city are Cubs fans (and go to the predominantly white jazz clubs!) while those from the south are White Sox fans (and frequent the black blues clubs!). The South Siders are equally as frustrated as baseball fans from the north, having had only one World Series appearance since just after the First World War.

Charter members of the American League, the White Sox play in the oldest ballpark in the United States, replete with the famous exploding scoreboard installed by former owner Bill Veeck. Currently situated alongside what was the largest railway stockyard in the world, the White Sox have ambitious plans to move their stadium, perhaps in consort with the Chicago Bears.

At one time the White Sox wore colourful Gay 90s uniforms, a turn of the century outfit with peaked pillbox caps. The players refused to complete the look by wearing shorts however!

Their proudest moment was back in 1906 when the White Sox won an all-Chicago World Series, beating the Cubs and disproving a nickname they had acquired earlier that season 'the Hitless Wonders'.

The first All-Star game was held at the White Sox home, Comiskey Park, in 1933 and the second in 1950.

In 1919 scandal struck, and that year's team will be remembered by baseball historians as the 'Black Sox'. Eight players were accused of being involved in a betting scandal and of deliberately throwing games in that year's World Series. Although found not guilty by the courts, they were banned for life by the Commissioner for baseball and, in effect, so were the club, who could not put together a side good enough to return to the World Series for forty years.

Finally, you would think us remiss if we didn't report that by all accounts the ladies' loos at Comiskey Park are the prettiest in major league baseball. But we have no first-hand knowledge of the facilities yet.

Carlton Fisk, the White Sox veteran catcher.

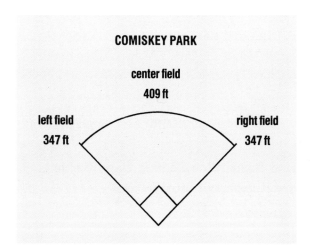

COMISKEY PARK

center field
409 ft

left field
347 ft

right field
347 ft

CHICAGO WHITE SOX
Comiskey Park
324 West 35th St
Chicago, Illinois 60616
Tel: (312) 924 1000

Stadium: Comiskey Park

Opened: 1 July 1910 (oldest ballpark in US)

Capacity: 44,087

Surface: Grass

World Series: Won 1906, 1917; lost 1919, 1959

Pitchers: Neil Allen (r), Floyd Bannister (l), Joel Davis (r), Jose DeLeon (r), Richard Dotson (r), Bob James (r), Joel McKeon (l), Ray Searage (l), Bobby Thigpen (r), Jim Winn (r)

Catchers: Carlton Fisk, Ron Hassey, Ron Karkovice

Infielders: Ozzie Guillen, Donnie Hill, Tim Hulett, Fred Manrique, Jerry Royster, Greg Walker

Outfielders: Harold Baines, Daryl Boston, Ivan Calderon, Jerry Hairston, Gary Redus

Manager: Jim Fregosi

CINCINNATI REDS
National League

★ ★ ★ ★ ★ ★

Charter members of the National League, Cincinnati are in fact baseball's oldest team because they formed a professional club way back in 1869, the Cincinnati Red Stockings, becoming the Reds seven years later. Their membership has not been continuous, however, because they were thrown out of the League in 1880 for the double crime of playing baseball and selling beer on Sundays. Their absence only lasted for four years and the Reds re-emerged still selling beer and playing ball on the seventh day of the week.

Acknowledged as the oldest club, the Reds are normally granted the honour of starting off each season with a home game on baseball's opening day. In 1987, however, Canadian Johnny-come-latelies the Toronto Blue Jays slipped a 1.30 start into their schedule to get in first, proving that even in baseball nothing is sacred. In fact, the Reds have been consistent pioneers in baseball, being instrumental in the first night game (when President Roosevelt switched on the first major league floodlights in 1935 without having to leave the comfort of the White House in Washington); organising the first regular radio coverage of a ballclub (1929); playing in the first televised game (1939); and being the first club to travel to a game by air (and therefore probably the first one to lose its luggage).

Pete Rose, now the Reds player/manager.

The club is owned by a consortium of local businessmen. Their stadium, the $48-million Riverfront Stadium, was opened in 1970 in the middle of the city on the banks of the Ohio River, and is a rather charmless product of the late-1960s fashion for civic project stadiums-in-the-round. The stadium is shared with the NFL's Cincinnati Bengals and for the baseball club serves as a replacement for the 1902 Crosley Field which had been one of America's most beautiful ballparks. You'll be interested and envious to know that when Crosley Park opened one could buy 12 beers for a dollar!

For years the Reds lived and died by the home run, the big hit in the big innings, but because their pitching could not match their batting the Reds were, historically, frequent 'unlucky' losers of 12-10 ballgames.

In the 1970s, a team of strong hitters and aggressive fielders emerged with star players Johnny Bench, Pete Rose, Joe Morgan, George Foster and Dave Concepcion all becoming members of the legendary Big Red Machine that won the National League in 1970, 1972, 1975 and 1976 and won the World Series in the last two of those years.

The aggressive tradition continues with Pete Rose back at Cincinnati as player/manager, the only dual role in the majors today and the first one for decades.

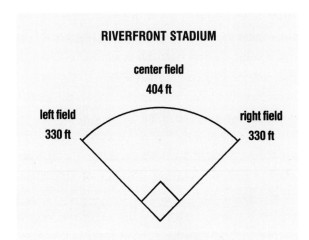

RIVERFRONT STADIUM

center field
404 ft

left field
330 ft

right field
330 ft

CINCINNATI REDS
100 Riverfront Stadium
Cincinnati, Ohio 45202
Tel: (513) 421 4510

Stadium: Riverfront
Stadium

Opened: 30 June 1970

Capacity: 52,392

Surface: Artificial grass

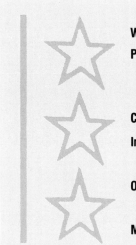

World Series: Won 1919, 1940, 1975, 1976; lost 1939, 1961, 1970, 1972

Pitchers: Tom Browning (l), John Franco (l), Bill Gullickson (r), Guy Hoffman (l), Bill Landrum (r), Rob Murphy (l), Ted Power (r), Ron Robinson (r), Frank Williams (r)

Catchers: Sal Butera, Bo Diaz, Lloyd McClendon

Infielders: Buddy Bell, Dave Concepcion, Terry Francona, Barry Larkin, Ron Oester, Kurt Stillwell

Outfielders: Kal Daniels, Eric Davis, Leo Garcia, Tracy Jones, Paul O'Neill, Dave Parker

Manager: Pete Rose

CLEVELAND INDIANS

★ ★ ★ ★ ★ ★

If you ignore the National Basketball Association's Cleveland Cavaliers (and most people do), Cleveland has been America's best-kept sporting secret. With the Cleveland Browns now firmly established as one of the strongest teams in the NFL, everybody is now tipping the Indians to be the 'surprise' team of the 1987 baseball season. All this for a modestly constructed city on the shores of Lake Erie, an hour or two's flight from New York.

The Indians were founder members of the American League, and play in the largest stadium in baseball, a 74,000-seat horseshoe-shaped monster that was built as part of Cleveland's unsuccessful bid to stage the 1932 Olympics. It's a big drafty place, in imitation of its home city, and is particularly cool in early and late season evening games. Although the stadium was completed in 1931, neither the Indians nor the Browns moved in until after the war, the Indians playing in their old League Park – one of six homes the club has had in its history. They've gone under different names too – Spiders, Blues, Bluebirds, Broncos and Naps before becoming Indians in honour of Louis Francis Sockalexis who, although sounding like a character from *Dynasty,* was the first Red Indian to play in major league baseball for Cleveland in the 1890s. Cleveland had the first black player in the American League and the first black manager too, Frank Robinson, who took charge in 1975 in a sport which has had a wretched record in giving top jobs to minorities. Cleveland also claims to be the rather unlikely inventor of the season ticket in baseball, and therefore probably in world sports, by introducing them for the 1871 season – $6 for a single

but $10 bought you tickets for yourself, your lady and your carriage.

The first event at Cleveland's spanking new Municipal Stadium was the 1931 fight between Max Schmeling and Young Stribling for the World Heavyweight Championship, but the Indians were in there just two weeks later and played there intermittently for the next 15 years – a mere 76,979 turning up for that first game. More than 86,000 watched the fifth game in the 1948 World Series at Municipal Stadium in Cleveland's last World Series-winning year.

Cleveland's first hero, back in the first year of the American League, was the joyfully named Napoleon Lajoie, who won the first year's batting championship in 1901, and stole 240 bases in an era before base-stealing became an art form. A later hero was pitcher Cy Young, after whom the annual 'Pitcher of the Year' award is named.

The Indians have been in just three World Series. In 1920 they beat the Brooklyn Dodgers. In 1948 their All-Stars were pitchers Bob Fuller and Bob Lemon, infielder Al Rosen (now general manager of the San Francisco Giants) and player/manager Lou Boudreau. They followed up a victory over the Boston Red Sox in a one-game play-off with one over the Boston Braves in the World Series. In 1954, they went down 4-0 to the New York Giants.

If the Cleveland Indians do turn out to be the team of the 1987 season, the names you will be hearing will be those of veteran pitchers Phil Niekro and Steve Carlton, along with one of the great characters of the game, Rick Dempsey, as one of the catchers and Cory Snyder, a star outfielder.

CLEVELAND MUNICIPAL STADIUM

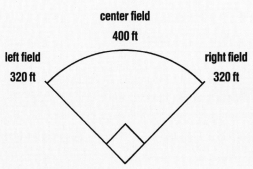

center field
400 ft

left field
320 ft

right field
320 ft

CLEVELAND INDIANS
Cleveland Stadium
Boudreau Blvd
Cleveland, Ohio 44114
Tel: (216) 861 1200

Stadium: Cleveland Municipal Stadium

Opened: 31 July 1931

Capacity: 74,028

Surface: Grass

Indians pitcher Phil Niekro.

World Series:	Won 1920, 1948; lost 1954
Pitchers:	Scott Bailes (l), Ernie Camacho (r), Tom Candiotti (r), Steve Carlton (l), Doug Jones (r), Phil Niekro (r), Ken Schrom (r), Greg Swindell (l), Ed Vande Berg (l), Tom Waddell (r), Rich Yett (r)
Catchers:	Chris Bando, Rick Dempsey
Infielders:	Tony Bernazard, Julio Franco, Brook Jacoby, Pat Tabler, Andre Thornton
Outfielders:	Brett Butler, Joe Carter, Carmen Castillo, Mel Hall, Otis Nixon, Cory Snyder
Manager:	Pat Corrales

DETROIT TIGERS

American League

Some of the largest American cities seem like ghost towns after six at night. As so few people now live in the downtown areas, once the commuters have headed for the suburbs the city seems to close down for the night. However, situated right in the middle of Detroit's downtown is fine old Tiger Stadium – built in 1912 and one of the great remaining traditional homes of baseball. Tiger Stadium keeps downtown Detroit buzzing during those long warm summer nights.

The stadium has undergone several reconstructions and name changes since the turn of the century – the last being in 1961 when Briggs Stadium became Tiger Stadium by merely investing in a T and an E and rearranging the neon letters. The stadium was the last of the American League clubs to install floodlights when in 1948 they installed eight towers providing 2,750,000 watts of light or, according to the more romantically inclined *Sporting News,* the equivalent of six thousand full moons!

An early batting hero in Detroit was one of the game's immortals, Ty Cobb, also known as the Georgia Peach. He took Detroit to three American League Championships in a row beginning in 1907, although his brilliant batting evaded him in the World Series and Detroit lost all three. He was twelve times batting champion of the American League and his *lifetime* average was .367 (remember that over .300 in a season is considered good).

Tigers pitchers Jack Morris (LEFT) and Mark Fidrych. Fidrych (nicknamed 'Big Bird' after a 'Sesame Street' character) scored the highest number of victories (19) by a Detroit rookie in 68 seasons in 1976.

Detroit failed again in the 1934 Series, but a year later were back in October to win their first world title beating their lakeland neighbours the Chicago Cubs, although they were losers again to the Cincinnati Reds in 1940.

Back in the World Series in 1945, wartime travel restrictions were still in force, and the first three games were scheduled at Detroit's home, the last four at the Chicago Cubs. The Tigers won this series to record their second success in nearly fifty years of trying. Two more victories followed – in 1968 the Tigers saw off St Louis, and then came a memorable season in 1984 when manager Sparky Anderson took the club to the American League Championship, winning it by a street, and to the World Championship. Anderson is the only manager to have won World Series with clubs from both Leagues, having managed the National League Cincinnati Reds to two World Series victories before taking the Tigers to their victory.

Visit Tiger Stadium if you are in Detroit and enjoy baseball in the fine old orange and navy blue surroundings of a stadium which reeks of baseball atmosphere.

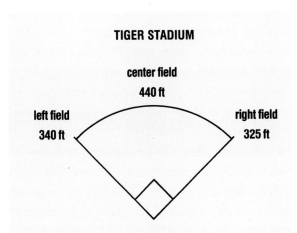

TIGER STADIUM

center field
440 ft

left field
340 ft

right field
325 ft

DETROIT TIGERS
Tiger Stadium
Detroit, Michigan 48216
Tel: (313) 962 4000

Stadium: Tiger Stadium

Opened: 1912

Capacity: 52,806

Surface: Grass

World Series: Won 1935, 1945, 1968, 1984; lost 1907, 1908, 1909, 1934, 1940

Pitchers: Willie Hernandez (l), Bryan Kelly (r), Eric King (r), Jack Morris (r), Dan Petry (r), Nate Snell (r), Frank Tanana (l), Walt Terrell (r), Mark Thurmond (l)

Catchers: Mike Heath, Dwight Lowry, Orlando Mercado, Matt Nokes

Infielders: Dave Bergman, Tom Brookens, Darnell Coles, Darrell Evans, Alan Trammell, Lou Whitaker

Outfielders: John Grubb, Terry Harper, Larry Herndon, Chet Lemon, Pat Sheridan

Manager: Sparky Anderson

HOUSTON ASTROS

National League

★ ★ ★ ★ ★ ★

The Astros began life as the Colt 45s when they and the New York Mets became the National League's newest clubs in 1962. When a new club is born it is allowed to participate in that year's 'draft' of college and other un-registered players, and is then allowed to raid the rosters of the other clubs – taking a couple of players from each team (other than a handful of stars who have been 'protected' by their clubs). The Mets went for ageing big names, the Colt 45s went for younger players grateful for a chance to make names for themselves. Neither policy proved to be particularly successful.

Trailed only by the comic-opera Mets and the suddenly inept Chicago Cubs, the 45s managed to finish eighth in their ten-team league in their first season. The Cubs quickly shook off the embarrassment of being beaten by an expansion team and from 1963 to 1968 Houston and New York shared bottom place in the league.

The climate in Houston in the summer is about the same as Bombay – hot and humid. So all the 45s' games were played at night in a small wooden stadium on the city's outskirts. The players and fans were somewhat distracted from the game by swarms of Texas-style mosquitos, 'the size of pigeons' according to manager Preston Gomez. The mosquitoes, not being particularly attracted by the standard of baseball, found the bright lights and captive flesh perfectly acceptable.

While the fans were beating off these airborne assaults with aerosol cans (throwing them at the mosquitos was one effective way of dealing with them) they could watch their team lose, consoled by the sight of a mighty building rising beyond the outfield, a great domed stadium. By now both the ballclub and the stadium had allied themselves with the nearby space centre and the Colt 45s became the Astros, and the new stadium became the Astrodome.

Everything in Texas is reputed to be the biggest in the world, and of course the Astrodome was and is the biggest in just about everything. Built at a cost of over $30 million, the stadium has 45,000 theatre-style seats. Two and a half million cubic feet of conditioned air circulates inside the Astrodome every minute and the stadium uses up a similar amount of electricity to a town of 9,000 people. Oh yes, and the plumbing can cope with 40,000 people washing their hands at the same time!

When it was opened in 1965 the Astrodome was immediately christened 'the eighth wonder of the world'. 'My rent is the ninth' commented the ballclub's owner soon afterwards. The eighth wonder, no doubt like the other seven, had its teething problems though. Outfielders tended to lose sight of the ball in the dome's transparent panels on sunny days. So, no problem, they painted the panels. The result was that with the sun cut off by the painted panels, the grass died. No problem, they invented Astroturf, a chemically based artificial grass that has plagued sport ever since (and gave rise to the joke about an American Football player who said, when asked whether he preferred Astroturf to grass: 'I don't know, I've never smoked Astroturf').

The Astros bounced between last place and next-to-last in the new western division throughout the 1970s. In 1980 they won their

Astros pitcher Nolan Ryan.

first divisional title, but were beaten by Philadelphia in the play-offs.

By 1986 they had developed a fine attacking ballclub led by Glenn Davis and Kevin Bass, and boasting All-Star pitching from fastball king Nolan Ryan and devastating split-fingered forkball pitcher Mike Scott.

The 1986 League Championship Series games against the Mets – both new clubs had now risen to the top – was one of the most exciting ever played. It was eventually won by the Mets when they won game 6, played in the Astrodome, by 7-6 in the 16th inning. Many people said it was the best game ever played, at least they did until they saw game 6 of the 1986 World Series ten days later!

The first indoor stadium, of course, meant the end of weather problems in baseball. That is until June 1976 when the players were trapped *inside* the stadium and the fans *outside* it by flooded streets after a torrential rainstorm – the first time a ball game was postponed because of wet ground outside the playing surface.

Finally, you'll be sorry to hear that the junior club associated with the Astros, which would normally also use that name, when playing in Kissimet (Florida) chose to use the name Osceola Astros rather than use the name of their real hometown. They couldn't change the Astros part of the name or they wouldn't be able to use hand-me-down shirts from the Houston club!

ASTRODOME

center field
400 ft

left field
330 ft

right field
330 ft

HOUSTON ASTROS

PO Box 288
Houston, Texas 77001
Tel: (713) 799 9500

Stadium: Astrodome (indoors)

Opened: 12 April 1965

Capacity: 45,000

Surface: Astroturf

World Series: None

Pitchers: Larry Andersen (r), Danny Darwin (r), Jim Deshaies (l), Charlie Kerfeld (r), Bob Knepper (l), Aurelio Lopez (r), Dave Meads (l), Nolan Ryan (r), Mike Scott (r), Dave Smith (r)

Catchers: Alan Ashby, Mark Bailey

Infielders: Glenn Davis, Bill Doran, Phil Garner, Jim Pankovits, Bert Pena, Craig Reynolds

Outfielders: Kevin Bass, Jose Cruz, Ty Gainey, Billy Hatcher, Davey Lopes, Terry Puhl

Manager: Hal Lanier

KANSAS CITY ROYALS
American League

★ ★ ★ ★ ★ ★

'We have traditional American values here – we like to get our children to school on time.' That remark by a resident of Kansas just about sums up the attitude of Americans in the Midwest. Another commented that: 'We are all meat and potato kind of guys here.' Kansas baseball reflects these values – hard-working value-for-money ballplayers playing the game for the entertainment of hard-working people who come to the ballpark looking to see value for their entertainment dollar. Men like George Brett typify the Midwest spirit; having been the mainstay of the Royals attack for ten years, in 1980 he nearly achieved the 'impossible' season average of .400 by hitting .390.

The Kansas City Royals were born in 1969, a year after the previous American League side in the city struck camp and made for Oakland in California. It was four years before the Royals had a palatial home to play in, but by 1973 the $70-million Harry S. Truman Sports Complex was ready to play ball in, and the well designed and equipped horseshoe-shaped stadium was open for business. Painted in the Royals' blue and white colours, the stadium boasted the first artificial surface in the league. A huge irony, since the Kansas groundskeeper, George Toma, was and is the foremost sporting grass expert in America, being responsible for the upkeep of the grass at every Super Bowl and most major baseball functions. At his home ground George just has to keep the Hoover well oiled and keep a variety of substances to neutralise the nasty things baseball players spit on to his plastic

Infielder George Brett.

carpet. Kansas has separately designed football and baseball stadiums right next to each other.

If the baseball ever gets boring in Kansas there is a 120-foot high electronic scoreboard and a giant waterfall that leaps higher in the air the more the crowd cheer. You could hardly be further away from a Sunday afternoon at Worcester, so never let anyone tell you baseball is like cricket!

Success for the Royals came comparatively quickly; they won their division in 1976, 1977, 1979 and 1980 and reached their first World Series in that last year. They lost to the infinitely more experienced Philadelphia, but were back in 1985 in a memorable World Series against the St Louis Cardinals.

The Cards and the Royals are separated by just two hundred miles of interstate motorway. The Series had such a lot going for it anyway that in a sense it hardly mattered how good the baseball was going to be. Kansas was known as the most easterly of the western clubs, St Louis the furthest west of the original eastern line up of clubs. Kansas had been in business fifteen years, St Louis had been around for a hundred years. The two mayors made the kind of deal guaranteed to increase the sporting rivalry – not only would the winning club's flag be flown from the losing town hall, but the winning mayor could govern the losing city for the day. Wouldn't that be unthinkable here in a Liverpool Cup Final?

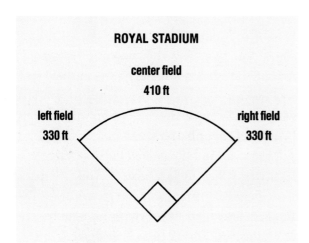

ROYAL STADIUM

center field
410 ft

left field
330 ft

right field
330 ft

KANSAS CITY ROYALS
PO Box 1969
Kansas City, Missouri 64141
Tel: (816) 921 2200

Stadium: Royal Stadium

Opened: 10 April 1973

Capacity: 40,625

Surface: Astroturf

World Series: Won 1985; lost 1980

Pitchers: Rick Anderson (r), Bud Black (l), Steve Farr (r), Mark Gubicza (r), Dave Gumpert (r), Danny Jackson (l), Charlie Leibrandt (l), Dan Quisenberry (r), Bret Saberhagen (r)

Catchers: Ed Hearn, Larry Owen, Jamie Quirk

Infielders: Steve Balboni, Buddy Biancalana, George Brett, Angel Salazar, Frank White

Outfielders: Juan Beniquez, Thad Bosley, Bo Jackson, Hal McRae, Jorge Orta, Kevin Seitzer, Danny Tartabull, Willie Wilson

Manager: Billy Gardiner

LOS ANGELES DODGERS

National League

★ ★ ★ ★ ★ ★

Any Brit who wants to experience the magic of modern American baseball, rather than wallow in its tradition, could do no better than to transport himself to Dodger Stadium. The Dodgers score highly on entertainment, razzmatazz, the Hollywood spirit, glamour, showbiz, spectacle and fun – and you can always live off the nationally famous Dodger Dog, the best hot-dog in American sport.

If there is such a thing as a downtown LA, the Dodgers have a prime piece of real estate right in the middle of it. A spectacular ravine location right in the heart of the city was the price the Brooklyn Dodgers extracted from Los Angeles in return for their sensational, to many heartbreaking, up and away from New York. To understand the impact of the move you would have to imagine a club like West Ham, with its deep working class East End roots, being moved almost overnight to Milton Keynes, or one of the proud traditional Lancashire clubs like Blackburn Rovers moved to Yorkshire. The Dodgers *were* Brooklyn, and anyway baseball was an eastern sport, wasn't it?

The Dodgers are the most colourful, individual and financially successful club in baseball. They have led the league in attendance figures since they moved from Brooklyn in 1957.

The team is owned by the O'Malley family. The late Walter O'Malley, father of the current club president, changed the game of baseball irreversibly from an eastern/mid-western one to the national pastime it is today when he went west and persuaded the New York Giants to come with him to California.

As the Brooklyn Dodgers from 1890 to 1957 (Dodgers as in 'trolley dodgers' – you had to be nimble to dodge between the speeding trolley cars that raced along Brooklyn's major thoroughfares at the turn of the century) the club didn't win pennants but their madcap players enjoyed a fanatical following for whom the phrase 'Wait until next year!' became an annual cry.

The tone was set for the atmosphere at the club when no one turned up with the keys of the ground when Ebbets Field was officially opened for play in Brooklyn, and they forgot to bring an American flag for the opening ceremony! Among the advertisements on the outfield wall was one for a local clothier: 'Hit this sign and win a suit' – an invitation taken up by many National League batters.

'Next year' finally arrived for the Dodgers in 1955 when they at last won a World Series – their only one from their Brooklyn base. The Dodgers beat their hated rivals from across the river, the New York Yankees, by 4 games to 3.

The transcontinentally transplanted Los Angeles Dodgers moved from Brooklyn's historic, cosy and idiosyncratic Ebbets Field to, of all places, the Los Angeles Coliseum, site of the 1932 and 1984 Olympics and then home of the LA Rams football team. Meanwhile historic Ebbets Field became a distinctly unhistoric housing estate.

The Coliseum was not exactly designed with baseball in mind – 450 feet to center and right field, but only 250 feet to the left-field stands, easy meat for a right-handed slugger. But if

Fernando Valenzuela, 1981 Rookie of the Year.

the ballpark was eccentric, it was also a money-spinner. It seated 100,000 people, and there were all those baseball-starved Angelinos to tempt into the ballpark, not to mention all those easterners who had come out west and had been separated from their favourite sport. Attendances soared to record heights. With one million a year being a good figure for most clubs, the Dodgers often clear *three* million.

As the money kept rolling in, in their second year in LA the Dodgers beat the Chicago White Sox in the 1959 World Series, setting attendance records that will never be beaten. The other major league teams that had moved their franchise in the 1950s had been losing money in their old cities – not so the Dodgers who had enjoyed a large, loyal following in Brooklyn, but played in a small ballpark. The shift to Los Angeles was simply a way to make a lot more money.

They had won the 1955 World Series in Brooklyn with an outstanding team, which went west with the rest of the furniture and fittings. Gil Hodges, Pee Wee Reese and Duke Snyder are all Hall of Fame players, but it was their two pitchers, the right-handed Don Drysdale and the left-handed Sandy Koufax, who captured Californian imaginations and made the players celebrities equal to the movie stars.

The Los Angeles Dodgers continued their success in the sunshine, winning the World Series in 1959, 1963, 1965 and 1981 and losing (usually to the Yankees) in 1966, 1974, 1977 and 1978. The later Dodgers used the base-running skills of Maury Wills and a phenomenal pitching find Fernando Valenzuela, a Mexican star who performs wonders on the mound and wondrous things for the attendance figures with the large hispanic population of Los Angeles.

Another Dodger 'character' is their manager Tommy Lasorda, an exuberant, colourful, highly visible leader. Tommy is the sports hero of Hollywood's elite and his office often rivals the Polo Lounge of the Beverly Hills Hotel for attracting the rich and famous. When the Dodgers win Tommy smiles and cheers. When they lose, he eats – his native Italian food, Chinese food, any food. He has a separate, larger wardrobe for losing streaks.

The Dodgers understood the American sports television market of the late 1950s and 1960s better than the other teams, and at a time when the majority of clubs sold local television rights to most of their games, the Dodgers restricted television to Sunday afternoon games and games against their old rivals the San Francisco Giants. They had brought their very popular commentators, headed by Vin Scully, with them from New York, and the limited number of broadcasts were treated as major events, and the advertising income from them was substantial. For the Dodger fan who wanted to see his team other than on Sundays, there were seats available to him at the stadium – all he had to do was bring the money! The Dodgers now have a successful pay-television operation in southern California.

Throughout this book you will read occasional references to injustices the sport of baseball has done to various racial minorities, a disgraceful undercurrent in a marvellous mainstream sport. Three cheers then for the Dodgers, who in the face of public opinion, and it should be said player opinion too, went out of their way to hire the first black player in major league baseball. They integrated baseball in 1947 with the signing of Jackie Robinson, who was promoted from their Montreal-based minor league team. Up to that momentous decision, there had been co-existing negro leagues, although some black players had made it to the major leagues, euphemistically called American Indians. Robinson was the official first, and it took a brave management to sign

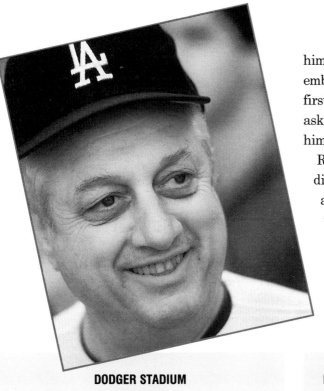

him and a brave team captain who publicly embraced Robinson on the field just before his first game for the Dodgers. Other players had asked to be traded rather than play alongside him.

Robinson overcame the rampant prejudice directed at him and became a star. A football and baseball player for UCLA, he turned out to be an exceptional batter, fielder, base-runner and eventually team leader for the Dodgers.

Tommy Lasorda, the Dodgers' exuberant manager.

DODGER STADIUM
center field
395 ft

left field
330 ft

right field
330 ft

LOS ANGELES DODGERS
1000 Elysian Park Avenue
Los Angeles, California 90012
Tel: (213) 224 1500

Stadium: Dodger Stadium

Opened: 10 April 1962

Capacity: 56,000

Surface: Grass

World Series: Won (Brooklyn) 1955; (LA) 1959, 1963, 1965, 1981; lost (Brooklyn) 1916, 1920, 1941, 1947, 1949, 1952, 1953, 1956; (LA) 1966, 1974, 1977, 1978

Pitchers: Orel Hershiser (r), Brian Holton (r), Rick Honeycutt (l), Ken Howell (r), Tim Leary (r), Tom Niedenfuer (r), Alejandro Pena (r), Jerry Reuss (l), Fernando Valenzuela (l), Bob Welch (r), Matt Young (l)

Catchers: Mike Scioscia, Alex Trevino

Infielders: Dave Anderson, Mariano Duncan, Jeff Hamilton, Bill Madlock, Steve Sax, Franklin Stubbs, Tracy Woodson

Outfielders: Jose Gonzalez, Pedro Guerrero, Ken Landreaux, Mike Marshall, Len Matuszek, Mike Ramsey, Reggie Williams

Manager: Tommy Lasorda

MILWAUKEE BREWERS

★ ★ ★ ★ ★

'What made Milwaukee famous made a loser out of me' goes the song, referring to the Schlitz beer which flows out of a Milwaukee brewery. What made the baseball team perennial losers is less certain.

There have been four quite different ballclubs in Milwaukee over the years, two American and two National League sides. An 1878 National League franchise only lasted one season. Milwaukee was a charter member of the American League in 1901 and again only lasted one season. The third attempt at making baseball pay in Milwaukee came with the transfer of the Boston Braves to the brewing city in 1953. The Braves adorned the first ballpark built with public money, County Stadium, and the crowds to begin with were good – in the first year in Milwaukee eight times as many fans watched the Braves as did in their last year in Boston.

Despite two World Series appearances – winning in 1957 and losing the following year – attendances fell away, and in 1965 the Braves decided to move on to the southern boom town of Atlanta.

The fourth team to try its luck in Milwaukee was born out of the ashes of the failed Seattle Pilots franchise which, after just one year in Seattle, moved to Schlitz country in 1970, becoming the Brewers.

The Brewers won the second half of the strike-divided 1981 season, but lost to the Yankees in the play-offs. The following year saw as close a race in the American League as there ever has been. The Brewers had a three-game lead over Baltimore with only four games to play. Those four games were against Baltimore! After the Orioles won the first three games the whole season was reduced to one game, the winners going on to the League Championship series. Milwaukee had acquired pitcher Don Sutton late in the season for just such a crisis and he led the team home in that fourth game 10-2. Milwaukee went on to that year's World Series before losing to the St Louis Cardinals in seven games.

In one of baseball's smallest cities, a game at County Stadium can be a fun family affair reflecting the German origins of the population. The ballpark serves a variety of bratwurst, liverwurst, weisswurst and any other kind of wurst or hot-dog you can think of. And as befits a brewing centre, it offers a wide selection of the cold stuff. There is a large beer barrel in center field and when a Brewer hits a home run, a little man glides down a slide into an artificial, alas, beer stein.

If baseball has had a rocky existence in the north-western state of Wisconsin, it does appear to be established there now. The Brewers' star player is outfielder Robin Yount.

At the start of the 1987 season Milwaukee fans had something unusual and a little ironic to cheer. The Brewers started the season like a greyhound out of the traps, winning a record-equalling thirteen games in a row. And who held the record with the Brewers? None other than the Braves, once a Milwaukee club and now settled in Atlanta. But, as if to prove that all silver linings have a cloud behind them, the Brewers then managed to lose ten games in a row!

Manager Tom Trebelhorn, a former Oakland Athletics player, joined the club in 1986.

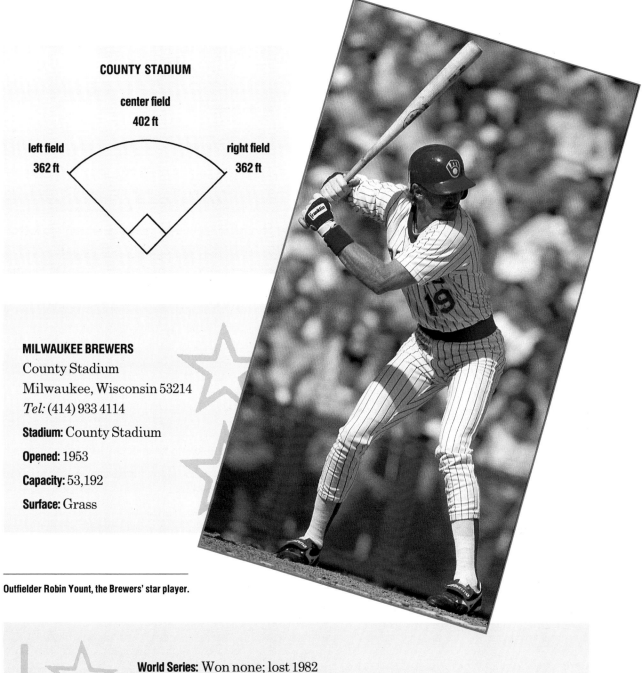

COUNTY STADIUM

center field
402 ft

left field
362 ft

right field
362 ft

MILWAUKEE BREWERS
County Stadium
Milwaukee, Wisconsin 53214
Tel: (414) 933 4114

Stadium: County Stadium

Opened: 1953

Capacity: 53,192

Surface: Grass

Outfielder Robin Yount, the Brewers' star player.

World Series:	Won none; lost 1982
Pitchers:	Mike Birkbeck (r), Chris Bosio (r), Mark Ciardi (r), Mark Clear (r), Chuck Crim (r), Teddy Higuera (l), John Henry Johnson (l), Juan Nieves (l), Dan Plesac (l), Bill Wegman (r)
Catchers:	Bill Schroeder, B.J. Surhoff
Infielders:	Greg Brock, Juan Castillo, Jim Gantner, Paul Molitor, Jim Paciorek, Billy Joe Robidoux, Dale Sveum
Outfielders:	Glenn Braggs, Rob Deer, Mike Felder, Rick Manning, Robin Yount
Manager:	Tom Trebelhorn

MINNESOTA TWINS

American League

★ ★ ★ ★ ★ ★

In an earlier life the Twins were the Washington Senators, charter members of the American League. A popular but in the early days not very successful side, the Senators won the World Series in 1924, but lost in 1925 and 1933. The lament 'Washington – first in war, first in peace and last in the American League' was a popular pre-war joke.

In its later years in Washington the team was owned by the Griffith family, well connected politically in the capital. The family and the ballclub were assured of one front-page picture each year because they generally persuaded the President to throw out the ceremonial first ball at the Senators' opening game.

The thing Calvin Griffith did best was save money – he even traded his son-in-law short stop Joe Cronin to the Red Sox when his salary demands became higher than Griffith thought reasonable.

Meanwhile in the north-western state of Minnesota, the two cities of Minneapolis and St Paul decided to try and attract a major league baseball club. They built a stadium with a capacity of 30,000 midway between the two cities, and drew crowds of over 20,000 for pre-season exhibition matches. In 1961 Griffith moved the Senators to the twin cities and renamed them the Minnesota Twins. The Bloomington ballpark was a lovely place to watch and play baseball – set in Minnesota farmland and blessed with grateful, loyal fans.

Twins outfielder Kirby Puckett.

The team prospered in their new surroundings, and in 1965 they reached the World Series, losing 4-3 to the Dodgers. In 1969 and 1970 they won their division, but lost to the Baltimore Orioles in the American League Championship.

The Twins in the 1970s had a clutch of really outstanding athletes, but most were allowed to continue their careers elsewhere so the club didn't have to pay the market rate for their services. Players like Harmon Killebrew, Ken Lamdreaux, Mike Marshall, Jim Kaat and their crown jewel Rod Carew, who was sent to the California Angels, all played for and left the Twins. The payroll at Minnesota became the league's lowest, but their scouting organisation was sound and new, and promising and cheaper

ball players were always coming up. Pitchers Bert Blyleven, Frank Viola and Jeff Reardon, infielders Greg Gaetti and Kent Hrbek and star outfielder Kirby Puckett are reasons why Minnesota still usually manages to be a contending team.

The Twins shared Metropolitan Stadium with the football Vikings – an even more successful enterprise – but the field was not ideal for football and frequently too cold for baseball. Both clubs moved to the new downtown domed Hubert H. Humphrey Metrodome stadium in 1982 – which is great for football but can be too hot for baseball! It's not a luxury stadium: 'The idea is to get the fans in, let 'em see a game and then let 'em go home' say the Twins.

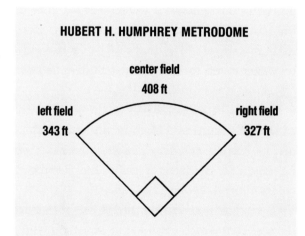

HUBERT H. HUMPHREY METRODOME

center field
408 ft

left field
343 ft

right field
327 ft

MINNESOTA TWINS

Hubert H. Humphrey Metrodome
501 Chicago Avenue South
Minneapolis, Missouri 55415
Tel: (612) 375 1366

Stadium: Hubert H. Humphrey Metrodome (indoors)

Opened: 6 April 1982

Capacity: 55,244 **Surface:** Artificial surface

World Series: Won none; lost 1965

Pitchers:	Keith Atherton (r), Juan Berenguer (r), Bert Blyleven (r), George Frazier (r), Mark Portugal (r), Joe Klink (l), Jeff Reardon (r), Mike Smithson (r), Les Straker (r), Frank Viola (l)
Catchers:	Tim Laudner, Tom Nieto, Mark Salas
Infielders:	Gary Gaetti, Greg Gagne, Kent Hrbek, Steve Lombardozzi, Al Newman
Outfielders:	Tom Brunansky, Randy Bush, Mark Davidson, Dan Gladden, Kirby Puckett
Manager:	Tom Kelly

MONTREAL EXPOS
National League

The Expos' Tim Raines.

The Expos and the San Diego Padres joined the National League in 1969. Montreal was the first major league team located outside the United States. The team is owned by the Bronfman family, owners of one of Canada's largest distillers (Seagrams etc.). The club may be Canadian but the players generally aren't – they've had only three in their history, all pitchers who did not last long with the club.

The team is nationally televised across Canada, but in the early years their games were played in Jarry Park, a 28,000-seat stadium in the suburbs. Everyone's expectations were realised when Montreal's first nationally televised game for the United States, against Cincinnati, was interrupted by snow!

Being in the heart of Quebec, the scoreboard, advertising signs and stadium announcements are in French and English, *en francais et en anglais,* and two sets of radio and television commentators follow Expo games.

The Expos, named after the 1967 World's Fair (Exposition) which was held in Montreal were, in their first year, started with unwanted players from other National League teams. They drafted better, more colourful players than San Diego and hired a first-class manager in Gene Mauch, long-time chief of the Philadelphia Phillies. The Expos were bottom of their division for two seasons, but they did have popular players like Rusty Staub (a redhead known as 'Le Grand Orange'), Maury Wills, Warren Cromartie and 'The Spaceman' – pitcher Bill Lee, who would occasionally wear his uniform backwards and claimed the brownies (biscuits) he brought with him to the ballpark were laced with marijuana (often the only real grass in the stadium).

In 1977, the Expos moved from cosy Jarry Park to the huge Olympic Stadium, a cold concrete mass with a bad artificial surface that has proved to be unpopular with both players and fans. The plans for the home of the 1976 Olympics called for a retractable cap for the top of the stadium to be suspended from a large column bending over it. There were delays in construction and ten years later it was still somewhere in France!

A roof was installed in 1987 – at a cost of $21 million – but its retractability will not be tested until the end of the 1987 baseball season.

The Expos have had enough good players in recent years to be regular contenders for the National League's eastern title. Success in 1987 depended on the successful re-signing of free agent Tim Raines.

There was a players' strike in 1981, and the leagues played a split season, with divisional winners before and after the strike playing off to decide the champions. The Expos won the second half of the season, beat the Phillies in the play-off, but lost to the Dodgers in the League Championship Series. That was as close as the Expos have come to a World Series, which has never been played outside the USA. Maybe manager Buck Rodgers will take the Expos into the twenty-first century!

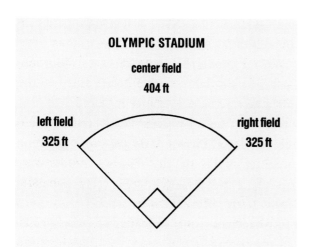

OLYMPIC STADIUM

center field
404 ft

left field
325 ft

right field
325 ft

MONTREAL EXPOS
PO Box 500, Station M
Montreal, Quebec
Canada
Tel: (514) 253 3434

Stadium: Olympic Stadium

Opened: 15 April 1977

Capacity: 59,149

Surface: Artificial surface

World Series: None

Pitchers: Bill Campbell (r), Neal Heaton (l), Bob McClure (l), Andy McGaffigan (r), Jeff Parrett (r), Randy St Claire (r), Bob Sebra (r), Lary Sorensen (r), Jay Tibbs (l), Floyd Youmans (r)

Catchers: Jeff Reed, John Stefaro

Infielders: Hubie Brooks, Casey Candaele, Tom Foley, Andres Galarraga, Wallace Johnson, Vance Law, Tim Wallach

Outfielders: Dave Engle, Reid Nichols, Alonzo Powell, Mitch Webster, Herm Winningham

Manager: Buck Rodgers

NEW YORK METS

★ ★ ★ ★ ★

The Mets are one of those ballclubs who never seem to do things by halves – after starting seasons of such ineptitude that a book was written about them called *Can't Anybody Here Play This Game,* there came the 1969 season when, as 100-1 outsiders, the Mets had their usual terrible start to the season but went on to win an amazing World Series.

And then came 1986 – the Mets won their division by more than 20 games and triumphed over Houston in the League Championship Series by winning the sixth game inside the Astrodome in a game which many believe to be the best game ever played. 'Just call it *the* game' said the Mets' Keith Hernandez. In the sixth game of the World Series the Mets were one out away from defeat and clawed their way to victory, the seventh game and the World Championship itself.

Short stop Rafael Santana put 1986 in perspective: 'It's different this year. Last year I'd wake up and the first thing I'd think about was "How are we going to win tonight?" This year the first thing I think about is breakfast!'

The New York Mets were born out of the vacuum that developed when both the Brooklyn Dodgers and the New York Giants fled the city for the West Coast in 1957. For six years America's largest city had no National League team and only one club – the American League's Yankees.

The Dodgers and the Giants had been involved in one of baseball's great rivalries, and the sudden and dramatic desertion to the New World of California was a devastating blow to fans in New York, and some observers believe that sport in America has not been the same

since. The Dodgers' relocation to Los Angeles and the Giants' move to San Francisco paved the way for the later moves of both New York's American football teams from the city of New York to nearby New Jersey, and the equally sudden and dramatic moves of the Oakland Raiders and Baltimore Colts football teams to Los Angeles and Indianapolis respectively. In this respect it seems government, both local and federal, can do nothing to stop big business when it decides to move a sporting club. The fans' opinion comes last – as it generally does on this side of the Atlantic too.

With Philadelphia now the only National League side left in the North-East – the birthplace of major league baseball – it was clear that another New York team would evolve. John Payson and his wife Joan, a daughter of the wealthy Whitney family, were granted a franchise to revive NL baseball in New York. The Paysons chose the name Metropolitans – only to find apparently serious objections raised by both the Metropolitan Museum of Modern Art and the Metropolitan Opera!

When a new team is elected to a league, as the Mets and Houston were in 1962, the other clubs protect their best players and then allow the newcomers to 'draft' players from those that are left. This is not a very generous arrangement and it is difficult to start a club from such beginnings. While Houston gambled on a collection of young up-and-coming players, the Mets, conscious of their New York heritage, turned first to big names, many of them

Lenny Dykstra in a 1986 Mets/Red Sox game.

decidedly over the hill, with whom to relaunch the sport in New York. Many of those names were former Dodgers and Giants, and they were managed by one of New York's most successful and famous coaches Casey Stengel, who had led the Yankees to three successive World Series victories. The Mets opened their major league career at the Polo Grounds, former home of the Giants, at the northern tip of the island of Manhattan, within sight of Yankee Stadium. By common consent those early Mets were the worst major league baseball team ever assembled. In their opening season the Mets managed to lose 120 of their 160 games, finishing a mere $60\frac{1}{2}$ games behind their division's leaders!

While the Mets struggled on the field, a new stadium was being constructed for them in the borough of Queens. Shea Stadium was built for the Mets and for the New York Titans of the American Football League, later the NFL's New York Jets. America discovered the Beatles, too, in a nationally televised concert from Shea in 1964.

From about 1967 things began to improve for the Mets. Their farm system (minor league clubs where young players develop) began to bring on young players of major league talent. Under the management of Gil Hodges, himself a former Met and Brooklyn Dodger, quality players like Tom Seaver and Nolan Ryan arrived to pitch the Mets towards glory. The year 1969 was that of the Amazin' Mets, a year when the club zoomed from laughing stock to World Champions. An astonishing late season run took the Mets from bottom of their division to divisional champions, pennant winners and World Series champions, beating the favourites, the Baltimore Orioles, by 4 games to 1.

During the 1970s the Mets were once more in transition. Gil Hodges died in 1971 and was replaced by one of the game's legends, Yogi Berra. Mrs Payson died and her husband elected to sell the Mets. The club was on the slide, with a losing team on the field and the fans staying away in their thousands. The new owners of New York's poor relation of baseball were the publisher Nelson Doubleday and the owner of the New York Islanders ice hockey team, Fred Wilpon. Frank Cashen, who had known great success at Baltimore, was the general manager charged with rebuilding the club from the farm system upwards. Out of that system came Darryl Strawberry, Lenny Dykstra, Mookie Wilson and Dwight Gooden – all of them stars on the 1986 World Series winning team. The catalyst who was responsible for turning these disparate stars into a championship-winning team was Davey Johnson, a former Baltimore Oriole, Atlanta Brave and Tokyo Giant who had never managed in the major leagues before. In 1984 the side looked promising; in 1985 they had clearly turned the corner, although they lost the National League pennant to the Chicago Cubs. In 1986, influential catcher Gary Carter celebrated his new $2 million-a-year contract by leading the Mets to their second World Series victory in a memorable series against the Boston Red Sox. It was a year in which everyone expected the Mets to win. They did. The regular batting order of Dykstra, Hernandez, Carter and Strawberry and a pitching rotation built around Dwight Gooden, Bob Ojeda, Ron Dar-ling and Jesse Oresco dominated the season from opening day. The team had a swagger which set it apart from the others, an arro-gance which annoyed other players in the league, and a will to dominate unusual in baseball. They were not a popular team outside New York.

The Mets are very much a product of their environment. New York is a bustling metropolis, a city which never closes, and home of the rich and famous. In much the same way as the average New Yorker thinks he knows everything, the Mets think they have it made. 'Baseball like it oughta be!' shout the banners which top Shea Stadium (or did, because they were soon replaced by '1986 World Champions', some say before the World Series started). Shea is in fact a run-down stadium which never found an acceptable compromise between football and baseball. Many of the baseball seats are too far away from the action, although the modern video screens and PA system offer an electronic buzz to the atmosphere of important games at Shea. When 60,000 people rock to the Queen song 'We will rock you' as the Mets win a World Series game, the experience is unforgettable.

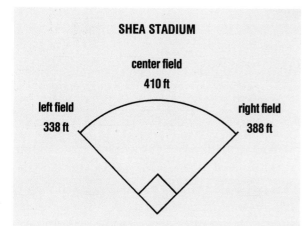

Mets pitcher Dwight Gooden.

SHEA STADIUM

center field
410 ft

left field
338 ft

right field
388 ft

NEW YORK METS
126th Street & Roosevelt Avenue
Flushing, New York 11368
Tel: (718) 507 6387 or 507 METS

Stadium: Shea Stadium
Opened: 17 April 1964
Capacity: 55,601
Surface: Grass

World Series: Won 1969, 1986; lost 1973

Pitchers:	Rick Aguilera (r), David Cone (r), Ron Darling (r), Sid Fernandez (l), Dwight Gooden (r), Terry Leach (r), Randy Myers (l), Bobby Ojeda (l), Jesse Orosco (l), Doug Sisk (r), Gene Walter (l)
Catchers:	Gary Carter, Clint Hurdle, Barry Lyons
Infielders:	Wally Backman, Keith Hernandez, Howard Johnson, Al Pedrique, Rafael Santana, Tim Teufel
Outfielders:	Lenny Dykstra, Lee Mazzilli, Kevin McReynolds, Darryl Strawberry, Mookie Wilson
Manager:	Davey Johnson

NEW YORK YANKEES

American League

★ ★ ★ ★ ★

This is baseball's most famous club, the Manchester United or Liverpool of American sport. You can see Yankee pinstripes worn all over the States, in Europe, Australia and in Japan. The classically elegant NY logo is seen on more baseball caps around the world than any other, and everywhere you go you will find Yankee fans. Most of the top names in the sport have worn the pinstripes – Babe Ruth, Joe DiMaggio, Mickey Mantle, Reggie Jackson, Dave Winfield. The Yankees have won a record 33 American League Championships, and a record 22 World Series – the next best World Series record is nine.

Outfielder Dave Winfield.

The Yankees' success had always been something of a problem for the American League until the 1960s – there have been the Yankees and seven other teams, and some of the 'other seven' have nearly gone under as a result.

As with so many other teams in baseball, the Yankees started in another town – Baltimore in 1901 – as a founder member of the American League. In 1903 the team was purchased for $18,000 and became the New York Highlanders, playing at Hilltop Park in upper Manhattan. They were bought to challenge the National League's popular New York Giants, and within ten years they had attracted a large enough following to outgrow Hilltop and make a ground-sharing arrangement with the Giants. The two teams played in Harlem's Polo Grounds, the Highlanders becoming the Yankees during the change of ground. In 1915 the beer baron Colonel Jacob Ruppert bought the team and dressed them in pinstripes, supposedly to cut down on cleaning bills and to make some of the players look slimmer! Since then the pinstripe look has been copied by many other teams (including the New York Mets) but they remain a Yankee trademark.

On 3 January 1920 the Yankees made the move that made the team a pre-eminent force – they purchased the young pitcher-fielder-hitter Babe Ruth from the Boston Red Sox. He was an instant star in New York, the most colourful figure in baseball at a time when it was most needed, just after the Chicago Black Sox betting scandal.

Everything Babe Ruth did seemed to be larger than life. His appetites were enormous; it seemed he patronised every restaurant in New York. For Ruth life was one long brunch – he even sent the clubhouse attendants out for hot - dogs and beer during the game, followed by glass after glass of bicarbonate of soda. You can still find autographed pictures of Babe Ruth in some of the older New York 'saloons' today.

He was recognised and fêted everywhere he went, and seemed genuinely to enjoy the perpetual spotlight. One Yankee who was told to share a room with Ruth on the road said: 'It wasn't a problem. I rarely saw him!' They say that Ruth was generous with his time, making hospital visits etc., and with his money, being a soft touch for anyone with a sob story. He was the highest paid ballplayer of his era, and when told that he was making more money than the President of the United States (Herbert Hoover) he said: 'Why not? I'm having a better year than he is!'

The popularity of Ruth and the Yankees made them uncomfortable tenants of the Giants, and in 1923 they moved just a few hundred yards across the Harlem River into a newly constructed Yankee Stadium: 'the House that Babe Ruth Built'. Before the first game in the new park, Babe Ruth told friends that he'd 'give up a year of my life if I could hit one today'. That afternoon he hit the first home run in Yankee Stadium to beat the Red Sox 4-1 in front of a crowd claimed to be 74,008. Actually the stadium couldn't hold that many fans, and the total was probably nearer 62,000. Attendance figures were not questioned very closely in those days. That unforgettable first season ended with the Yankees proudly winning their first World Series – beating their rivals from over the river, the Giants, by four games to two.

In June the following year, Yankee first baseman Wally Pipp was replaced in a game by a young second-year player named Lou Gehrig. Lou would play the next 2,130 consecutive games at first base, a record that will never be broken. That's fourteen years without missing a game through illness, injury or loss of form. Ironically, the illness that eventually broke the streak killed Gehrig within two years. He hit over 400 home runs, ten in World Series games, and won the league's Most Valuable Player nomination three times.

The Yankees, the first team to have their players wear numbers, retired Gehrig's No 4 and Ruth's No 3 and those of ten other players through the years. Except for a period during the 1960s, the Yankees have always been champions or contenders. After the Ruth–Gehrig era came other great stars – Joe DiMaggio, Phil Rizzuto, Whitey Ford, Don Larson and Yogi Berra.

Over the years there have been a number of great records set in Yankee Stadium. Babe Ruth hit his record-setting 60th home run in a single season there in 1927, and Roger Maris broke that record there in 1961. Don Larson pitched the first and only perfect game in a World Series in Yankee Stadium in 1956, and Joe DiMaggio began his 56-game hitting record there in 1941. Altogether Babe Ruth hit a record (broken in 1974) 714 home runs in his career.

The Yankees of the 1950s and early 1960s, managed by Casey Stengel, were probably the strongest team in baseball history. Led by Mickey Mantle, Yogi Berra and Whitey Ford the Yankees won the World Series in 1950, 1951, 1952, 1953, 1956, 1958, 1961 and 1962, and were beaten finalists in five other seasons between 1955 and 1964.

The ownership of the New York Yankees had been as consistent as the team – well-known winners. But in 1964 the CBS television network bought the team for over $14 million. The network was successful, but the team sank to the bottom of the league. In 1973 CBS sold out, at a loss, to a group headed by the current owner George M. Steinbrenner III, a Cleveland shipbuilder. Steinbrenner has not been one to operate in the background – in fact he is better-known than most of his players. Noting his dictatorial manner (Steinbrenner runs the club with a committee of 'baseball people' who once included a football coach!), the New York press dubbed him George III.

Steinbrenner arrived at about the same time as free agency, the means by which a player can sign with any other team once his current contract expires. Steinbrenner wanted a championship quickly, and having eyed the CBS failures in previous years, he set about tempting free agents with huge salary cheques. He acquired outfielder Dave Winfield from San Diego, pitchers Jim 'Catfish' Hunter from Oakland and Tommy John from Los Angeles; Rickey Henderson came from Oakland, and Lou Piniella from Cleveland. Joe Niekro came from Houston and Willie Randolph from Pittsburgh. In 1977 George III signed a young pretender – the brilliant slugger Reggie Jackson from Oakland via Baltimore. Jackson, never a modest character, called himself 'The straw that stirs the drink' when he joined the Yankees. The press and fans soon dubbed him 'Mr October' after he led the Yankees to World Series victories in 1977 and 1978.

George M. Steinbrenner's tendency to criticise players and managers in the press has been one of the most interesting cabarets in New York of recent years. When players play the game in a different way to George's ideas they are sacked – hence Reggie Jackson's departure in his prime to the California Angels and relief pitcher Goose Gossage's trade to San Diego. However, the greatest casualties have come in the manager's office. There have been *nine* managers since Steinbrenner took over the club, some lasting only weeks in the job. Actually there have been *fifteen* changes because George sometimes re-hires the last but one guy he sacked! Billy Martin has endured surely the ultimate love-hate relationship with an owner, having been re-hired four times!

When asked by Hugh McIlvanney on a Channel 4 programme whether he perhaps didn't understand the 'poetry of baseball', Steinbrenner snapped: 'Don't talk to me about poetry, I majored in English and there's nothing about Sheats and Kelly that I don't know.' Wouldn't Alf Ramsey have been proud of that?

YANKEE STADIUM

center field
410 ft

left field
379 ft

right field
353 ft

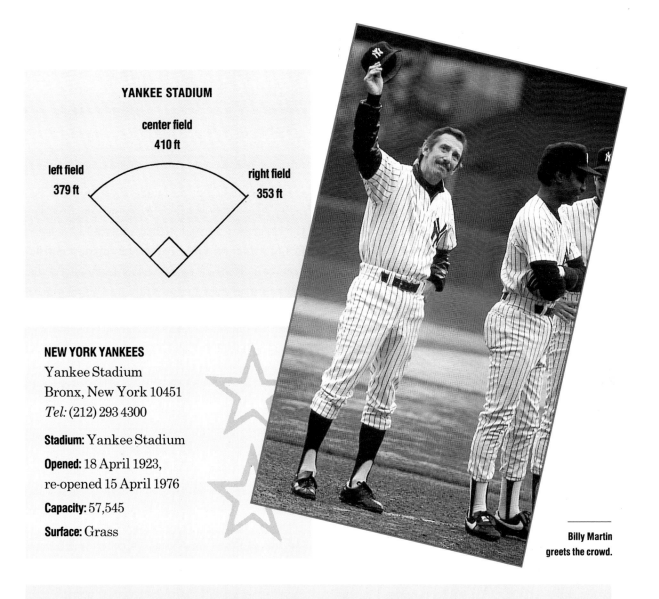

Billy Martin
greets the crowd.

NEW YORK YANKEES

Yankee Stadium
Bronx, New York 10451
Tel: (212) 293 4300

Stadium: Yankee Stadium

Opened: 18 April 1923,
re-opened 15 April 1976

Capacity: 57,545

Surface: Grass

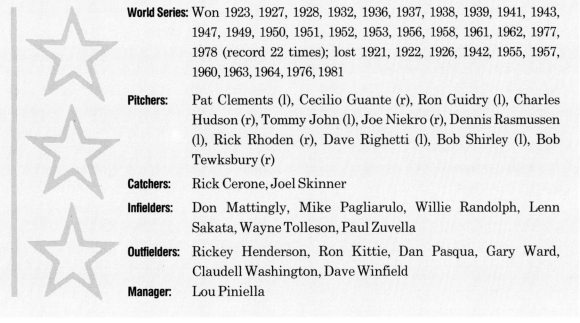

World Series: Won 1923, 1927, 1928, 1932, 1936, 1937, 1938, 1939, 1941, 1943, 1947, 1949, 1950, 1951, 1952, 1953, 1956, 1958, 1961, 1962, 1977, 1978 (record 22 times); lost 1921, 1922, 1926, 1942, 1955, 1957, 1960, 1963, 1964, 1976, 1981

Pitchers: Pat Clements (l), Cecilio Guante (r), Ron Guidry (l), Charles Hudson (r), Tommy John (l), Joe Niekro (r), Dennis Rasmussen (l), Rick Rhoden (r), Dave Righetti (l), Bob Shirley (l), Bob Tewksbury (r)

Catchers: Rick Cerone, Joel Skinner

Infielders: Don Mattingly, Mike Pagliarulo, Willie Randolph, Lenn Sakata, Wayne Tolleson, Paul Zuvella

Outfielders: Rickey Henderson, Ron Kittie, Dan Pasqua, Gary Ward, Claudell Washington, Dave Winfield

Manager: Lou Piniella

THE OAKLAND ATHLETICS

Oakland is the poor man's San Francisco, situated just across the bay from one of the world's most beautiful cities. It is the home of what passes for heavy industry in California, and an important military base – the last sight of America for many servicemen *en route* to the Pacific theatre of war and to Vietnam.

The Oakland Coliseum, home to the NFL Raiders until they migrated to Los Angeles, has been home to the Athletics since the team moved west in 1968. The Athletics, or 'A's to give them their more popular title, are a transcontinental three-town franchise. They were the Philadelphia Athletics from 1901 to 1955, rather faceless Kansas City Athletics from 1955 to 1968 and the remarkable, colourful and sometimes successful Oakland 'A's from then to now.

The club was owned and managed by Connie Mack from its founding in 1901 to his retirement half a century later. He won five World Championships in that time, and since he was his own boss he will probably always have the longest serving manager record!

In the late 1960s, the 'A's were sold to insurance magnate Charles O. Finley, while he was making a living in the Midwest city of Kansas. The 'O', he claimed, stood for 'owner'. Finley was an innovator and a visionary. The 'A's were the first club to break away from the traditional and seemingly mandatory white uniforms at home and grey on the road.

He built a giant computerised scoreboard at the Stadium, and began pushing for World Series games to be played under lights at night. He bought a mule for a mascot, which he kept in an enclosure in center field: 'The mule is smarter than most of my players,' he said.

In Oakland, the 'A's made their home debut on 17 April 1968 against the Baltimore Orioles. In the crowd of over 40,000 was the Governor Ronald Reagan who threw out the ceremonial first ball. In that first season Catfish Hunter pitched a perfect game, and the 'A's began to look like a team ready for honours.

Led by the hitting of the immortal (if you don't take our word for it, you'll take his) Reggie Jackson, the 'A's won three consecutive World Series, beginning in 1972 – only the Yankees had ever achieved this before. Dick Williams managed two of these great sides before resigning after the 1973 success.

In the late 1970s the 'A's couldn't get anything right, while their fellow tenants at the Coliseum, the Oakland Raiders, coached by John Madden and Tom Flores, became one of the dominant forces in the National Football League. In 1979, the 'A's lost 108 games, and once attracted only 653 spectators. Meanwhile Finley sold the team to the jeans' manufacturers Levi-Strauss.

Enter Billyball, a fast exciting strategy designed by manager Billy Martin, a four times member of the George Steinbrenner fan club (see NY Yankees). Billyball involved speedy running and daring base stealing, an all-action entertainment centred around the basestealing skills of Ricky Henderson. In 1982 Henderson broke the major league basestealing record with a month of the season still to play, ending with 130 bases stolen.

In 1987, the 'A's signed a promising free agent who, as a designated hitter, just might cause some impact this season. His name? Reggie Jackson, freed by the California Angels.

OAKLAND COLISEUM

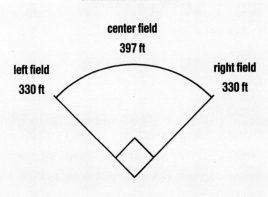

center field
397 ft

left field
330 ft

right field
330 ft

OAKLAND ATHLETICS

Oakland Coliseum
Oakland, California CA 94621
Tel: (415) 638 4900

Stadium: Oakland Coliseum

Opening game: 17 April 1968

Capacity: 50,219

Surface: Grass

Reggie Jackson joined the Athletics in 1987.

World Series:	Won (as Philadelphia 'A's) 1910, 1911, 1913, 1929, 1930; (as Oakland) 1972, 1973, 1974; lost (as Philadelphia 'A's) 1905, 1914, 1931
Pitchers:	Chris Codiroli (r), Dennis Eckersley (r), Jay Howell (r), Bill Krueger (l), Gene Nelson (r), Steve Ontiveros (r), Eric Plunk (r), Jose Rijo (r), Dave Stewart (r), Curt Young (l)
Catchers:	Terry Steinbach, Mickey Tettleton
Infielders:	Ron Cey, Alfredo Griffin, Carney Lansford, Johnnie LeMaster, Mark McGwire, Rob Nelson, Tony Phillips
Outfielders:	Jose Canseco, Mike Davis, Reggie Jackson, Stan Javier, Dwayne Murphy
Manager:	Tony LaRussa

PHILADELPHIA PHILLIES
National League

★ ★ ★ ★ ★

For a brief time in the early 1980s, Philadelphia was the sporting capital of the USA, with winning teams in baseball (the Phillies), in football (the Eagles), in basketball (76ers) and in ice-hockey (the Flyers). Given also that Philadelphia is quite an attractive city steeped in history, and with a proud record in the War of Independence, it was not a bad place to be, sports fan or not.

The Phillies were charter members of the National League in 1876. They were, though, at one time known as the Blue Jays and played in a small park where practically any fly ball had the potential to make itself a home run!

For most of their life in baseball, until the mid-1950s, the Phillies were Philadelphia's second team, behind the popular Athletics of the American League, who were always in contention for championships. The Phillies did win one National League title – in 1915 – but lost the World Series to the Boston Red Sox. Their next Series appearance was not until 1950 when their 'Whizz Kids' team beat Brooklyn to the National League title, but again lost the World Series, this time to the Yankees.

Philadelphia fans are loyal, and love a winner in any sport, but they can't take losers. 'OK, they boo us,' said one umpire. 'But then they boo both teams and the National Anthem singer. If they saw it, they'd probably boo the sunrise!'

In 1964, the fans had plenty to boo – at one time the Phillies were well on the way to the National League Championship. In September they led by nine games, but with just two weeks of the season left, there came The Great Fold. They lost ten of their last twelve games to finish an unseemly second. The hair of their manager,

Gene Mauch, turned grey and some of the players thought seriously about wearing their batting helmets home.

The Phillies moved to their all-purpose synthetic grass Veterans Stadium in 1977. The team improved considerably with stars such as Pete Rose, Tony Perez, Tim McCarver and their all-time leader in everything – runs scored, games played, runs batted in, total bases, extra base hits etc. – Mike Schmidt. Their pitching star was Steve Carlton, 'Lefty' to his fans. Angered by the Philadelphia press, which was as unruly as the fans, he refused to talk to anyone but his team-mates for several years. Through his catcher and friend Tim McCarver, NBC once offered Carlton, a wine connoisseur, a case of wine of his choice in return for a short interview. McCarver came back with a quick 'yes'. But there was no interview because NBC discovered just in time that the case of wine chosen by Carlton would have cost them $20,000!

The Phillies won their first World Series, indeed their first World Series game, in 1980 when they defeated Kansas City by four games to two. They were National League champions again in 1983, but lost the Series to Baltimore. The fans and the writers found their usual way to express their appreciation of what, ultimately, was another losing season.

If you're ever in Philadelphia on the season's opening day, the ceremonial pitch is always worth watching. The Phillies have a tradition of something unusual – dropping the ball from a helicopter, shooting it out of a cannon or having it delivered on horseback are all variations on an entertaining theme.

VETERANS STADIUM

center field
408 ft

left field
330 ft

right field
330 ft

PHILADELPHIA PHILLIES

PO Box 7575
Philadelphia
Pennsylvania, PA 19101
Tel: (215) 463 6000

Stadium: Veterans Stadium

Opened: 10 April 1971

Capacity: 66,271

Surface: Artificial grass

Steve 'Lefty' Carlton, Phillies pitching star of the 1970s.

World Series:	Won 1980; lost 1915, 1950, 1983
Pitchers:	Steve Bedrosian (r), Don Carman (l), Joe Cowley (r), Kevin Gross (r), Tom Hume (r), Mike Jackson (r), Shane Rawley (l), Bruce Ruffin (l), Dan Schatzeder (l), Kent Tekulve (r)
Catchers:	Lance Parrish, John Russell
Infielders:	Luis Aguayo, Von Hayes, Steve Jeltz, Juan Samuel, Mike Schmidt, Rick Schu
Outfielders:	Mike Easler, Greg Gross, Chris James, Ron Roenicke, Milt Thompson, Glenn Wilson
Manager:	John Felske

PITTSBURGH PIRATES

National League

★ ★ ★ ★ ★ ★

America's former great steel town, the visual inspiration for the film *Flashdance,* Pittsburgh sits in the old industrial north-east trying to keep up with the booming cities of America's Sun Belt. The Pirates' Three Rivers Stadium sits in sporting isolation in the industrial heart of the city, an old club in a new stadium in a rebuilding city.

Pittsburgh's industrial heritage comes in part from its position at the confluence of the two great rivers that join forces there to make the Ohio River. The stadium takes its name from this major feature. The Pittsburgh area has made its sporting impact on the rest of the USA because there are Pittsburgh men on the rosters of all the major league baseball and football teams.

The Pirates were a dominant team in the first quarter of the century, winning World Series in 1909 and 1925, and being beaten finalists in 1903 and 1927. Honus Wagner was their first big star, in the early 1900s. The Pirates played in the first-ever World Series, in 1903, and won the 1909 Series, but it must all have seemed like ancient history as the club struggled through the 1930s, 1940s and 1950s with very little for the fans to cheer about.

After the war, the local hero was Ralph Kiner, the perennial National League batting and home run champion, but the team had few other good players and very weak pitching. Thus the Pirates lost a lot of exciting 8-7 and 10-9 ballgames.

By the early 1960s the Pirates had rebuilt with pitchers Bob Friend, LeRoy Face and Vernon Law, and fielders Dick Groat, Bill Mazeroski and the electric Roberto Clemente, who was

National League batting champion in 1961, 1964, 1965 and 1967. Clemente was in his prime as a player when he was killed in a plane crash on a Christmas rescue flight to victims of a hurricane in Nicaragua in 1972.

The 1960 World Series against the New York Yankees was as exciting as any played, won by Pittsburgh 4-3 on Bill Mazeroski's ninth-inning home run.

In 1970 the Pirates left comfortable Forbes Field for the new, round, synthetic-turf Three Rivers Stadium, shared with the NFL's famous 'steel curtain' football team, the Pittsburgh Steelers, who won the Super Bowl four times in the 1970s.

A new crew of Pirates powered the team to World Series victories over Baltimore in 1971 and again over the same opposition eight years later. They won both series by 4 games to 3, having recovered from being two games down in 1979. These new Pirates included Dave Parker, Bill Matlock and Willie Stargell, who wore the orange and black with distinction. The first-ever World Series game to be played at night was part of that 1971 Series, enabling television viewers all over the country to see the game in prime time.

In the 1980s the Bucs (derived from buccaneers, as in pirates) went backwards again. League position and attendances fell until in 1986 the Pirates won 64 and lost 98 games, the worst record anywhere in major league baseball.

During the close season the Pirates traded for three bright young pitching hopefuls to go with their anchoring pitcher Rick Reuschel in the hope of more success in 1987.

Pirates pitcher Rick Reuschel.

THREE RIVERS STADIUM

center field
400 ft

left field
335 ft

right field
335 ft

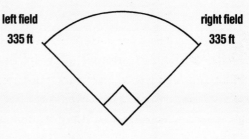

PITTSBURGH PIRATES
600 Stadium Circle
Pittsburgh
Pennsylvania 15212
Tel: (412) 323 5000

Stadium: Three Rivers Stadium

Opened: 16 July 1970

Capacity: 58,438

Surface: Artificial grass

World Series: Won 1909, 1925, 1960, 1971, 1979; lost 1903, 1927

Pitchers: Doug Drabek (r), Logan Easley (r), Brian Fisher (r), Barry Fisher (r), Barry Jones (r), Bob Kipper (l), Bob Patterson (l), Rick Reuschel (r), Don Robinson (r), John Smiley (l), Bob Walk (r)

Catchers: Junior Ortiz, Mike LaValliere

Infielders: Bill Almon, Rafael Belliard, Sid Bream, Onix Concepcion, Jim Morrison, Johnny Ray

Outfielders: Barry Bonds, Bobby Bonilla, John Cangelosi, Mike Diaz, R.J. Reynolds, Andy Van Styke

Manager: Jim Leyland

ST LOUIS CARDINALS

National League

★ ★ ★ ★ ★

Owned by the beer baron Gussie Busch, the St Louis Cardinals play in Busch Stadium, an all-purpose beer park built in the 1960s and shared with the football club of the same name. Possessing a hard, unpopular artificial surface, the park is right in the middle of St Louis, near the Mississippi and the city landmark of Gateway Arch.

Before the Dodgers and Giants moved from New York to the West Coast in the late 1950s, St Louis was the furthest west of the baseball teams – in the old days a two-day train ride from the East Coast. The city is known as the most westerly city in Eastern America (Kansas being the most easterly in the west!). From the earliest radio days, St Louis broadcast on a powerful, clear station that could be heard all over the Midwest from the Canadian border all the way down to the Gulf of Mexico – the Cards are still one of the nation's best-loved teams. They are second to the Yankees in World Series success, winning nine of their fourteen appearances.

The Cardinals have an impressive World Series record, having won it nine times in 60 years, a level of consistency bettered only by the Yankees. Star of the 1926 win was a 39-year-old pitcher with the colourful name of Grover Cleveland Alexander. In 1931, the hot streak belonged to Pepper Martin, whose 12 hits took the Cards to their second World Series victory.

The 1930s Cardinals rejoiced under the name of the Gashouse Gang, who included the Dean brothers, Dizzy and Daffy. These great characters pitched for St Louis in the 1934 World Series-winning year, winning 49 games between them, 30 of them by Dizzy – the last time a National League pitcher won 30 games in a

season. It was during the 1934 Series that Daffy was sent to hospital after being hit on the head. 'It's OK,' he reported on returning to the team hotel, 'they X-rayed my head and couldn't find anything in it.'

During his later broadcasting career Dizzy Dean was berated by a listener for his poor grammar on the air: 'You don't even know the King's English,' she complained.

'Old Diz knows the King's English,' he answered, 'and not only that, I also know the Queen is English.'

Further wins came in 1942, 1944 and 1946 but the 1950s were barren, despite St Louis boasting at that time one of the game's great batters in Stan 'the Man' Musial, who started his career as a pitcher but went on to play in twenty All-Star games as a batter and once hit a record six home runs in one All-Star game.

The Midwest has blazing hot days, and sometimes chilly nights – all part of a day's work for the baseball player. After the All-Star game had been held in temperatures of 105°F in the new Busch Memorial Stadium in 1966, the National League manager Casey Stengel was asked his opinion of the new ballpark: 'Well, I must say it sure holds the heat well,' he replied.

The current St Louis manager is Whitey Herzog who during the 1987 season won his 1,000th victory as a manager, in this his 13th year in charge of a major league club. His 1985 Cardinals won more games than any other in the major leagues that year, and only lost a hotly contested World Series to Kansas City in the seventh game. He was also in charge when the Cardinals won in 1982, the last time a St Louis side won the World Series.

Having reached the World Series in 1985, where they lost to the Kansas City Royals, the Cardinals found 1986 a disappointing year, as they lost three more games than they won, ending up third in their six-team division.

Cardinals coach Whitey Herzog.

BUSCH STADIUM

center field
414 ft

left field
330 ft

right field
330 ft

ST LOUIS CARDINALS
250 Stadium Plaza
St Louis, Missouri 63102
Tel: (314) 421 3060

Stadium: Busch Stadium
Opened: 12 May 1966
Capacity: 50,222
Surface: Artificial grass

World Series:	Won 1926, 1931, 1934, 1942, 1944, 1946, 1964, 1967, 1982; lost 1928, 1930, 1943, 1968, 1985
Pitchers:	Danny Cox (r), Bill Dawley (r), Bob Forsch (r), Rick Horton (l), Dave LaPoint (l), Greg Mathews (l), Pat Perry (l), Ray Soff (r), John Tudor (l), Todd Worrell (r)
Catchers:	Steve Lake, Tom Pagnozzi
Infielders:	Rod Booker, Jack Clark, Mike Fitzgerald, Tom Herr, Mike Laga, Tom Lawless, Jim Lindeman, Jose Oquendo, Terry Pendelton, Ozzie Smith
Outfielders:	Dennis Carter, Vince Coleman, Curt Ford, Tito Landnum, Willie McGee, John Morris, Andy Van Slyke
Manager:	Whitey Herzog

SAN DIEGO PADRES

National League

They say that San Diego was a small fishing village when the National League was founded just over a century ago. Now it is a thriving Californian resort, a gateway to – or, more accurately, from – Mexico, and a light industrial city of great potential. In sports, the city lost its basketball team to Los Angeles and sometimes looks like losing its baseball team. San Diego hosts Super Bowl XXII in 1988.

The Padres are one of the National League's two newest teams, having been admitted with the Montreal Expos as expansion franchises in 1969. As expected from a team made up of hand-me-downs from other teams in the league, the Padres finished last in each of their first six years. They didn't do much better in the next eight years either, as fans generally found the beaches more attractive than the sporting entertainment on offer at the Jack Murphy Stadium. (Jack Murphy was a San Diego sportswriter.) It even looked as if the team might move to Washington, before it was bought by the man behind the McDonalds hamburger chain, Ray Kroc.

The first game he attended as owner was a typical Padre exercise in futility – so Mr Kroc got on to the public address system and said so. He called the team the worst he had ever seen and apologised to the fans for the lack of effort they had just witnessed. This caused a morale problem for the players, not to say a mutiny from men who would have been happy to see Mr Kroc placed between two buns and served with a portion of fries. Kroc was kept away from a microphone from that day onwards.

The famous San Diego chicken.

The team acquired some decent ballplayers and got rid of their nasty flashy uniforms. Dave Winfield played in San Diego, Steve Garvey came from the Dodgers, Craig Nettles and Goose Gossage caught the red eye from New York and surprise, surprise the Padres beat the Chicago Cubs in the 1984 National League play-offs before losing their only World Series to the Detroit Tigers by four games to one.

If the Padres seem to have a completely new team each year, it's largely the work of their general manager 'Trader' Jack McKeon, who trades players at the drop of a dollar bill. The success ratio on trades is probably slightly in the other teams' favour, but Jack keeps things moving along. Kevin McReynolds is this season's offering to the rest of the league – presented to the New York Mets in return for three of New York's brighter prospects.

Ray Kroc is dead now, and the club is owned by his widow.

Jack Murphy Stadium has been holding a maximum of 55,000 fans, and is modern and comfortable. It is being upgraded to accommodate 70,000 seats in time for Super Bowl XXII.

Having enjoyed Dodger Dogs, Fenway Franks, nachos at Arlington, sausages at Candlestick or crabcakes at Baltimore – when in San Diego do ask the locals if you can have a piece of San Diego chicken!

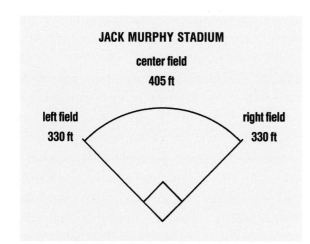

JACK MURPHY STADIUM

center field
405 ft

left field
330 ft

right field
330 ft

SAN DIEGO PADRES
9449 Friars Road
San Diego, California 92108
Tel: (619) 283 7294

Stadium: San Diego/Jack Murphy Stadium
Opened: 8 April 1969
Capacity: 58,433
Surface: Grass

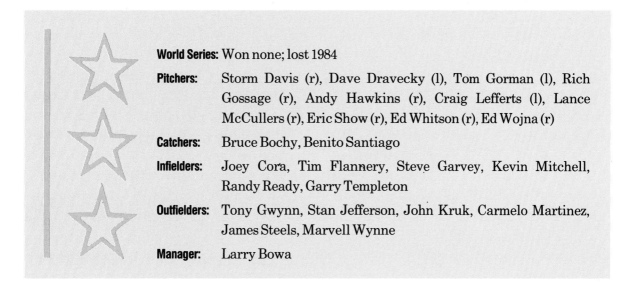

World Series: Won none; lost 1984
Pitchers: Storm Davis (r), Dave Dravecky (l), Tom Gorman (l), Rich Gossage (r), Andy Hawkins (r), Craig Lefferts (l), Lance McCullers (r), Eric Show (r), Ed Whitson (r), Ed Wojna (r)
Catchers: Bruce Bochy, Benito Santiago
Infielders: Joey Cora, Tim Flannery, Steve Garvey, Kevin Mitchell, Randy Ready, Garry Templeton
Outfielders: Tony Gwynn, Stan Jefferson, John Kruk, Carmelo Martinez, James Steels, Marvell Wynne
Manager: Larry Bowa

SAN FRANCISCO GIANTS

National League

★ ★ ★ ★ ★

When Walter O'Malley decided to move his Brooklyn Dodgers to Los Angeles in 1957, he needed another National League side to 'go West young man' with him. Otherwise travel expenses and schedule disruptions were likely to rule out his ambitious plans. The six teams remaining in the East and Midwest would be more likely to come out to California for two series of games than for one. O'Malley concentrated his efforts on Horace Stoneham, owner of the New York Giants. O'Malley shrewdly kept his idea of going to Los Angeles, while passing off San Francisco to his cross-town rival. The Dodgers were rewarded with instant success in LA, while the Giants settled into a less successful, acrimonious life in the Bay City.

The New York Giants were for years New York's and the National League's pre-eminent team. Charter members in 1876, there were Giants in New York before there were Dodgers, Yankees or Mets. From their New York base, the Giants played in fourteen World Series, winning five, the last in 1955 against the powerful and heavily favoured Cleveland Indians. The Giants' centerfielder Willie Mays made a catch in the first game off a towering 460-foot drive from Cleveland's Vic Wertz, crashing into the wall as he took the ball from over his shoulder. The disbelieving Indians made reservations to go home after crashing out by four games to none. In 1962 the Giants again beat the Dodgers in a play-off, and again qualified to meet the Yankees in the World Series. This time the Giants lost again in a series that had so many rain-outs in San Francisco it looked as if the World Series might finish after the Super Bowl.

You have to have been to Candlestick Park to conceive of how cold it is. Sitting there in beautiful Californian sunshine it is hard to believe it would be possible to construct a ballpark that attracts winds that feel like they've come straight off the Great Lakes. The wind was more or less a private baseball joke until the nationally televised All-Star game in 1961, when a typically crisp Candlestick Park breeze blew pitcher Stu Miller off the mound as he was about to pitch. Rick Friendrich of the *San Francisco Chronicle* has chilling memories of the Candlestick wind. He wrote: 'Winds of incredible cunning sometimes bear with gale force from home plate toward left field at ground level, while 100 feet above they bear from left field toward home plate at velocities that break out small craft warnings from the Coast Guard.'

In the 1970s the stadium was enlarged and enclosed around the outfield to accommodate the footballing 49ers and – hooray, hooray – the artificial grass was replaced with the real thing.

As the Giants fell to the bottom of the league, and attendances began to fall, they attempted to get out of Candlestick. The American League had moved a team into nearby Oakland where more typical Californian weather existed. The Giants even had a look at Toronto but again the American League got there first. Local politicians stopped the Giants building a new stadium in the draught-free downtown. The disillusioned Stoneham family, one of baseball's oldest, gave up and sold out to San Francisco real estate manager Robert Lurie, who has promised to get the team out of Candlestick Park but to keep them in the San Francisco area. While all the real estate moves have been going on the Giants, with the help of Roger Craig, the master and teacher of the split-fingered fastball, are improving on the field and are once more contenders – the players of course preferring to play road games!

The gourmet visitor to Candlestick Park should remember to wrap up warm, and however warm it is when he gets to the stadium should ignore the hot-dogs and beer and make straight for the fiery Polish sausages and the Californian wines!

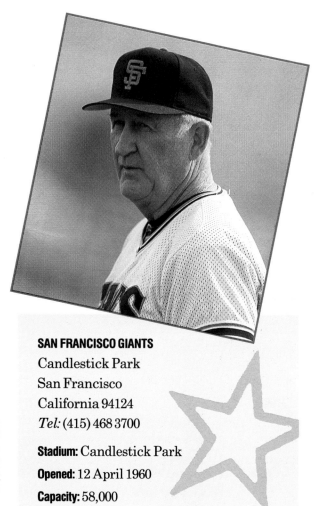

Giants manager Roger Craig.

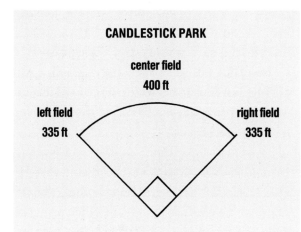

CANDLESTICK PARK

center field
400 ft

left field
335 ft

right field
335 ft

SAN FRANCISCO GIANTS
Candlestick Park
San Francisco
California 94124
Tel: (415) 468 3700

Stadium: Candlestick Park
Opened: 12 April 1960
Capacity: 58,000
Surface: Grass

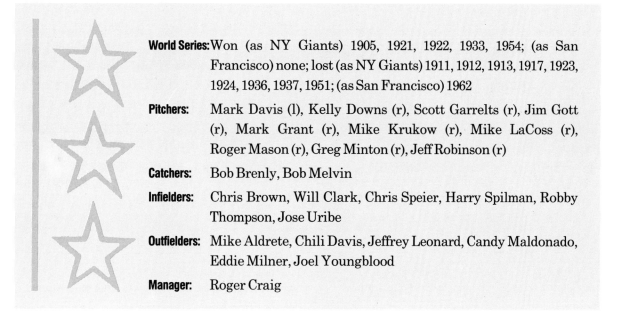

World Series:	Won (as NY Giants) 1905, 1921, 1922, 1933, 1954; (as San Francisco) none; lost (as NY Giants) 1911, 1912, 1913, 1917, 1923, 1924, 1936, 1937, 1951; (as San Francisco) 1962
Pitchers:	Mark Davis (l), Kelly Downs (r), Scott Garrelts (r), Jim Gott (r), Mark Grant (r), Mike Krukow (r), Mike LaCoss (r), Roger Mason (r), Greg Minton (r), Jeff Robinson (r)
Catchers:	Bob Brenly, Bob Melvin
Infielders:	Chris Brown, Will Clark, Chris Speier, Harry Spilman, Robby Thompson, Jose Uribe
Outfielders:	Mike Aldrete, Chili Davis, Jeffrey Leonard, Candy Maldonado, Eddie Milner, Joel Youngblood
Manager:	Roger Craig

SEATTLE MARINERS
American League

★ ★ ★ ★ ★ ★

A sign at the Florida Spring training headquarters of the Seattle Mariners reads: 'Seattle Mariners – 1987 World Champions'. As a piece of motivation, even Brian Clough wouldn't dare make so bold. As a prediction, don't even think about it!

In many ways Seattle is America's best-kept secret. Situated right up in the top left-hand corner of the United States, in the heavily forested state of Washington, Seattle has a lifestyle that most would envy. The countryside is beautiful, the coast and islands are spectacular, Alaska is there to be cruised to, and Vancouver is just a couple of hours drive over the Canadian border.

For sports fans there is the consistently reasonable NFL franchise the Seahawks, an NBA basketball team the Supersonics, and an American League baseball team which provides value for not much money, but has won no pennant or World Series yet.

An earlier attempt to establish baseball in Seattle failed after just one season when the Seattle Pilots spent the 1969 season losing a fortune before moving on to Milwaukee. The current Mariners are a team without much of a past, an uninspired present and an uncertain future. Seattle won its second expansion team in 1977, along with Toronto, so they are one of baseball's two newest teams. The Mariners

Mariners infielder Rey Quinones (formerly of the Red Sox) and (INSET) manager Dick Williams.

finished just ahead of their induction partners Toronto in that first season and have been near the bottom of the American League's Western Division–at sixes and sevens–every season since.

Seattle's manager is the veteran Dick Williams (the sixth to hold the position in ten years) who guided Boston, Oakland and San Diego to past World Series. He has few talented players to work with, two of the best, Dave Henderson and Spike Owen, having been traded to Boston in time to win World Championship medals there last season. The Red Sox player sent in the opposite direction, Rey Quinones, threatened to give up baseball rather than have to play for Seattle.

The Mariners play in the Kingdome, one of the nicer covered stadiums, built in 1977 at a cost of $67 million. The late comedian Danny Kaye was an earlier owner in the franchise.

The Mariners draw low attendances, not enough to meet the terms of their lease at the Kingdome, or to pay high salaries to the players, not enough in fact, to pay for a successful ballclub. Owner George Argyros is said to be contemplating selling the club. If the Mariners are sold, the chances are that the team will be moved in 1988 to either Denver or Phoenix, both cities clamouring for major league baseball. Wouldn't it be appropriate if out of the ashes of the Mariners there arose a Phoenix?

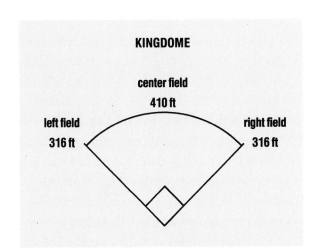

KINGDOME

center field
410 ft

left field
316 ft

right field
316 ft

SEATTLE MARINERS
PO Box 4100
Seattle, Washington 98104
Tel: (206) 628 3555

Stadium: Kingdome (indoors)

Opened: 6 April 1977

Capacity: 59,438

Surface: Artificial grass

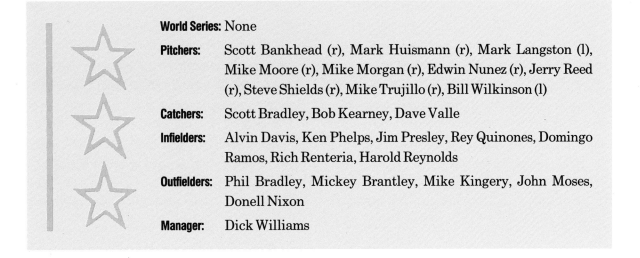

World Series: None

Pitchers: Scott Bankhead (r), Mark Huismann (r), Mark Langston (l), Mike Moore (r), Mike Morgan (r), Edwin Nunez (r), Jerry Reed (r), Steve Shields (r), Mike Trujillo (r), Bill Wilkinson (l)

Catchers: Scott Bradley, Bob Kearney, Dave Valle

Infielders: Alvin Davis, Ken Phelps, Jim Presley, Rey Quinones, Domingo Ramos, Rich Renteria, Harold Reynolds

Outfielders: Phil Bradley, Mickey Brantley, Mike Kingery, John Moses, Donell Nixon

Manager: Dick Williams

TEXAS RANGERS

American League

★ ★ ★ ★ ★ ★

We were once shown, in Dallas, what Texans proudly described as the biggest hole ever dug in the ground (it later became a hotel). If a thing isn't the biggest and best, Texans don't look twice at it, and that philosophy means that the Rangers have got to become a big noise in baseball if they are going to survive. Conveniently, and far from accidentally, situated midway between the cities of Dallas and Fort Worth, Arlington Stadium is the home of the fast-improving Rangers.

If you're reading this guide alphabetically you will be confused to learn that the Texas Rangers used to be known as the Washington Senators. Hang on, didn't they become the Minnesota Twins? Well, yes and no. The *original* Senators (1901-61) moved to Minnesota in 1961 but were immediately replaced by a new franchise in Washington which used the same name. These *second* Senators lasted in the nation's capital for just eleven years before heading south for Dallas.

The new Senators, owned by Robert Short, drew close to a million spectators a year – which is the sort of break-even mark which most clubs aspire to. They had some good players: a third base-short stop combination of Aurelino Rodriguez and Ed Brinkman, and a very large, very strong first baseman called Frank Howard. Howard led the team in home runs, total base hits, walks... and strike outs. In other words, he either missed the ball or hit it a very long way! The Senators had three distinguished managers while in Washington – James 'Mickey' Vernon, an old Senators hero, Gil Hodges, who had been a star for the Dodgers in both Brooklyn and Los Angeles, and was later to manage the Mets

to a World Championship, and Ted Williams, arguably the best hitter ever – the last player to average better than .400 in a season, a former Red Sox and an excellent teacher of the game.

Mr Short, who had a tendency to trade any players who came good for the club, decided that Dallas, Texas would be more profitable base for his team. The club, however, never reached Dallas, but, renamed the Texas Rangers after the state police force, started playing in Arlington.

Ted Williams was still the manager when the Rangers began playing in 1972, but after one season he gave it up and returned to his other love, fishing. He was succeeded by Whitey Herzog, who is now the highly successful manager of the St Louis Cardinals. Next came Billy Martin, who stopped over after managing in Minnesota and Detroit before becoming a frequent manager of the New York Yankees.

Martin pushed the Rangers to their best record ever, and second place in American west. The same year Bob Short sold the club to Texan industrialist Brad Corbett. From 1974 to 1986 the club drifted, generally downwards, and changed managers almost every year. In 1984 they hired a former player Tom Grieve as General Manager/Vice President and he brought in former Dodger, Angel and Met Bobby Valentine to manage.

Valentine has a string of restaurants in his native Connecticut and now in Texas, but his main concern is turning round the Texas ballclub. He has a young and enthusiastic team with infielder Pete O'Brien, outfielders Pete Incaviglia and Oddibe McDowell, veterans Larry Parrish and Tom Paciorek, and a good pitching staff led by former Dodger Charlie Hough.

In 1986 the Rangers led their division for a time but were finally beaten out by the California Angels. If the Rangers can find the confidence to beat the Angels with any regularity, they could win what is a comparatively weak division.

One record unlikely to be beaten was established at the Rangers Arlington Stadium in 1973, when Frank Robinson, then a veteran Angel, homered to complete a set of 32 ballparks in which he had scored runs. He had scored in some of the extinct places like Ebbets Field, the Polo Grounds, Connie Mack Stadium, the Los Angeles Coliseum and most of the current ones, too.

Knuckleball pitcher Charlie Bough, formerly a Dodger, now the leading Rangers pitcher.

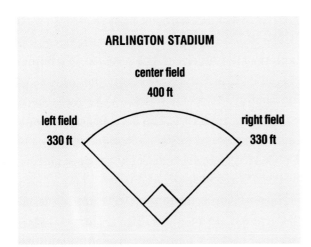

ARLINGTON STADIUM

center field
400 ft

left field
330 ft

right field
330 ft

TEXAS RANGERS
PO Box 1111
Arlington, Texas 76010
Tel: (817) 273 5000

Stadium: Arlington Stadium

Opened: 21 April 1972

Capacity: 43,508

Surface: Grass

World Series: None

Pitchers: Scott Anderson (r), Edwin Correa (r), Jose Guzman (r), Greg Harris (r), Charlie Hough (r), Mike Loynd (r), Mike Mason (l), Dale Mohorcic (r), Mitch Williams (l), Bobby Witt (r)

Catchers: Geno Petralli, Darrell Porter, Don Slaught

Infielders: Jerry Browne, Steve Buechele, Scott Fletcher, Pete O'Brien, Tom Paciorek, Larry Parrish, Curtis Wilkerson

Outfielders: Bob Brower, Pete Incaviglia, Oddibe McDowell, Ruben Sierra

Manager: Bobby Valentine

TORONTO BLUE JAYS

American League

★ ★ ★ ★ ★ ★

The Blue Jays were hatched in 1977, along with the Seattle Mariners – baseball's two youngest clubs. Seattle was needed to balance the schedule, and the League, at fourteen clubs, two more than the National League, but the important city in the expansion was Toronto. The National League already had one Canadian city in operation, Montreal, and were planning to move the San Diego club to Toronto to create a natural rivalry north of the border. The American League moved quicker than the National League and got in first – a move that has paid dividends in the last ten years.

The Blue Jays' first six years were spent at the bottom of the American League East. Their fans stayed loyal and the team began to improve – to fourth in 1983, second in 1984 and to the Eastern championship in 1985. The Blue Jays then lost a nail-biting League Championship Series to the Kansas City Royals, and Canada missed getting its first World Series by a whisker.

Toronto built its team on strong pitching, particularly from Dave Stieb, their all-time winning pitcher and team leader in innings pitched, earned run average, strike outs and shut outs. The young Californian became a Canadian sport hero.

Toronto is far from being a warm weather city, particularly in the spring and autumn, and the Blue Jays share old Exhibition Stadium, a 44,000-seat open park on the Canadian National Exhibition Grounds right on Lake Ontario, with the Argonauts of the Canadian Football League. Of course it snowed on their opening

Blue Jays pitcher Dave Steib (LEFT) and (RIGHT) Rance Mullinks, with California Angel Bob Boone.

home game, but they still won it. But fear not, another domed stadium is on the way – hopefully in time for a Toronto World Series, because games played up there outdoors in late October will be c-c-c-cold.

The Blue Jays' new home will be in downtown Toronto, will seat 58,000 and will feature a retractable 7,500-ton roof. What it will not feature, however, is parking space, although the stadium authorities say there are 15,000-17,000 spaces within half a mile or so of the ballpark. The *Toronto Star* thinks half an *hour* is more likely, and whoever heard of a North American walking that long, particularly in the snow!

The Toronto Blue Jays have the best outfield in baseball, but lack the pitching to be champions. Star performances from batters Jesse

Barfield, George Bell, Lloyd Moseby and Tony Fernandez must be matched by better pitching from Jimmy Key, Dave Stieb and Mark Eichhorn if the Canadian club is to improve on 1986's fourth place in their seven-team division.

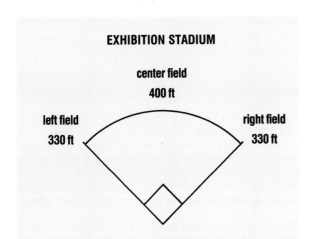

EXHIBITION STADIUM

center field
400 ft

left field   right field
330 ft   330 ft

TORONTO BLUE JAYS
Box 7777
Adelaide Street PO
Toronto, Ontario M5C 2K7
Canada
Tel: (416) 595 0077

Stadium: Exhibition Stadium

Opened: 7 April 1977

Capacity: 43,737   **Surface:** Artificial grass

World Series: None

Pitchers: John Cerutti (l), Jim Clancy (r), Mark Eichhorn (r), Tom Henke (r), Joe Johnson (r), Jimmy Key (l), Jeff Musselman (l), Jose Nunez (r), Dave Stieb (r), Duane Ward (r)

Catchers: Matt Stark, Ernie Whitt

Infielders: Tony Fernandez, Cecil Fielder, Kelly Gruber, Garth Iorg, Fred McGriff, Rance Mullinks, Mike Sharperson, Willie Upshaw

Outfielders: Jesse Barfield, George Bell, Rick Leach, Lloyd Moseby

Manager: Jimy Williams

GLOSSARY

★ ★ ★ ★ ★ ★

Assist A credit awarded to a fielder when his throw enables a teammate to make an out.

At bat The team or player batting is said to be 'at bat'.

Balk An illegal pitching motion, usually one which is stopped too late. It entitles all runners at bases (except the batter) to advance one base. A runner at third base will therefore score.

Ball A pitch which is outside the strike zone and is not swung at by the batter. If the pitcher throws four balls to the batter, the batter can have a free pass (or walk) to first base.

Base hit A hit into fair territory allowing the batter to reach first base before the fielding side can return the ball to their first baseman (also known as a single). Bigger hits result in doubles (reaching second base), triples (reaching third base) and home runs.

Base on balls Achieved by a batter who has received four balls and may proceed to first base.

Bases loaded The situation when there are runners at the first, second and third bases. If a batter makes contact now, he will hope to bring third base home (one run), perhaps second base too (two runs), even first base home for three runs. If he hits a home run with bases loaded his side will score a Grand Slam, four runs (one from each base and one by himself).

Batter's box The rectangle measuring six feet by four feet in which the batter must keep both feet while batting.

Batting average The number of hits divided by the number of times at bat. Expressed to three decimal places – .300 means three hits in every ten turns at bat; .400 has not been achieved in years.

Bleachers The public seats in the outfield, so-called because originally they were wooden and bleached by constant exposure to the sun.

Bullpen An enclosure where relief pitchers warm up.

Bunt A push with the bat that drops the ball close to the batter and gives him a chance to reach first base, or advances base runners because the fielder is likely to have a difficult throw to any base.

Called game A game in which the senior umpire abandons play, usually for rain. If a game is 'called' before the middle of the fifth inning it is replayed (usually when the visitors are next in town). When games are called after the middle of the fifth inning, the result stands.

Count The current state of play from the point of view of the batter. It is customary to give the count as two numbers, e.g. 'three and two' meaning three balls and two strikes.

Designated hitter A specialist batter who does not field, but takes the place of the pitcher in the batting line-up (also known as DH). It applies to the American League only.

Double A hit which carries the batter around to second base.

Double header Two games presented to the spectator for the price of one, one game between two clubs being almost immediately followed by another. Obviously the pitchers change, but otherwise the players are the same. Not only cynics feel that this value-for-money idea is rapidly disappearing from major league base-ball.

Double play The act of getting two runners out on one play. For example, a ball played to first base to get the batter out, might then be thrown quickly to third base to beat the man running from second.

Earned run A run which counts against the pitcher in his averages.

Earned run average (ERA) The total number of runs scored off a pitcher over a season divided by the number of innings he has pitched, and multiplied by nine. A pitcher's ERA is therefore the number of runs he is likely to give away in a full game. Under three is considered to be a good ERA.

Error Mistakes in the field which are charged to a fielder.

Extra innings Played when a game is tied after nine innings. Play continues until one team is ahead at the end of an equal number of innings, or when the team batting second takes the lead (26 innings is the record).

Fair ball A ball hit into fair territory, i.e. between the foul lines.

Fair territory That part of the field in front of the batter and between the foul lines and the batter. Runs and hits can only be scored when the ball is hit into fair territory. Note, however, that a batter can be caught anywhere, even in foul territory and even if a fielder can get into the crowd's seats to make a catch!

Fly ball A ball which comes off the round part of the bat and flies high in the air.

Force play Two runners cannot occupy the same base. A runner arriving at an occupied base is out.

Foul ball A ball which lands in foul territory. Foul balls count as strikes, except for the third strike, i.e. a batter cannot be struck out off a foul ball. Note that a batter can be caught off a foul ball.

Foul territory The area behind the batter and lines drawn from home plate to first base and third base. Batters can be caught in foul territory but cannot score hits or runs there.

Grand slam A home run hit when the bases are loaded, i.e. with a runner on each of the bases. A spectacular sight, as four runners come home scoring a run each.

Hit A proper contact with the ball by the batter, who successfully advances to first base.

Hit by pitch When a batter is hit by an errant pitch he is entitled to move to first base. Some batters specialise in this and can lean in to a pitch and get hit as many as thirty times a season, worth thirty base hits in other circumstances.

Home run The equivalent of a six in cricket, a ball hit cleanly over the boundary fence. The hitter and any runners on base each score a run. It is popularly called a 'homer'.

Infield The area contained by the four bases and their fielders (the infielders).

Inning Just to confuse the cricket fan, in baseball there are two half innings in an inning – each team having fielded and batted for one inning each. There are normally nine innings in a game, extra innings being played in the event of a tie.

Intentional walk A tactic in which a pitcher will allow a batter to advance to first base by throwing four wide balls, giving him no chance to hit and do more damage. It is usually a sign of respect for a batter who is likely to get a hit, but can be a threatening gesture to the batter who is next up implying that the pitcher thinks he is easier meat. It can also be used to set up a double play. This happens when there are men on base and two outs needed to end the inning.

On-deck circle A circle marked out in front of each team's dug-out. The next batter in warms up here in order to speed things up. If you get the opportunity to watch the batter on deck you will see he often watches the pitcher in action and swings as if he were facing him. This helps get his timing right when it is his turn to bat.

Passed ball A ball that is thrown by the pitcher, left or missed by the batter, and that the catcher then fails to catch. A runner can then advance.

Pinch hitter A substitute batter introduced into the game at crucial moments. The man he replaces, who is frequently a pitcher, can take no further part in the game.

Pinch runner A fast runner introduced to replace a man already on a base. The replaced player cannot return to the game.

Runs batted in (RBI) A figure used to measure the effectiveness of batters – it is the number of runs scored while he is at bat (remembering that a base hit by him might mean one, two or three runs are scored by other people already on base).

Sacrifice A play in which a batter concedes an out to advance a runner.

Stolen base When a runner at first or second base runs to the next base without waiting for a hit from the batter, he steals a base. Done behind the pitcher's back, it is a spectacular sight when achieved successfully. The batter can run at any time, but will be out if the pitcher or catcher gets the ball to the base ahead of him. Even more spectacular is a steal from third base to home – rarely attempted but perfectly legal.

Slugging percentage The total number of bases achieved by all base hits divided by the total number of games played.

Strike A pitch that falls within the strike zone and is not hit by the batter.

Strike zone The area over the home plate, which, in the batter's natural stance, is between the batter's knees and armpits, and in which any pitch is a strike.

Switch hitter Unbelievably, to someone brought up on cricket, some batters are equally effective batting left-handed or right-handed – taking up an appropriate stance according to whether the pitcher is left-handed or right-handed. A current exponent of switch hitting is Pete Rose of the Reds; a former star who could, so to speak, swing both ways was Mickey Mantle.

Tagging An infielder in possession of the ball touching a runner between bases.

Wild pitch The equivalent of a wide in cricket. Runners on bases are allowed to move up one base.

Won-lost percentage The number of games won by a team divided by the total number of games played, expressed to three decimal places.

BRITISH BASEBALL

★ ★ ★ ★ ★ ★

During 1987 the Scottish Amicable Life Assurance Society has backed the formation of a National Baseball League at venues throughout Britain. Local league baseball is played all over the country.

The Scottish Amicable National Baseball League Teams and Managers

HUMBERSIDE COUNTY BEARS
Don Smallwood
197 Newbridge Road
Hull HU9 2LR
Tel. (0482) 76169

Venue
Quibell Park Stadium
Brunby Wood Lane
Scunthorpe

LANCASHIRE RED SOX
Ken Dulson
4 Astley Close
Ramford
Lancashire
Tel. (074 488) 3405

Venue
Preston North End
Football Club
Deepdale Road
Preston
Lancashire

LONDON WARRIORS
Alan Smith
110 Barnsbury Road
London N1 0ES
Tel. 01-278 8706

Venue
Richmond Athletic Ground
Kewfoot Road
Twickenham Road
Richmond
Surrey

MERSEYSIDE MARINERS
Norman Wells
71A Mill Lane
Churchtown
Southport
Tel. (0704) 24846

Venue
Southport Football Club
Haig Avenue
Southport
Lancashire

NOTTINGHAM KNIGHTS
Alan Goodhead
11 Danes Close
Arnold
Nottingham
Tel. (0602) 203432

Venue
Wilford Sports Complex
Gresham Close
West Bridgford
Nottingham

SOUTHERN TIGERS
Peter Hunt
Flat 4
44 Redcliffe Gardens
London SW10
Tel. 01-937 6054

Venue
Richmond Athletic Ground
Kewfoot Road
Twickenham Road
Richmond
Surrey

British Baseball Federation Contacts

EAST MIDLANDS
Alan Goodhead
11 Danes Close
Arnold
Nottingham
Tel. (0602) 203432

HUMBERSIDE
Lachlan Forbes
43 Grantham Avenue
North Bransholme
Hull
Tel. (0482) 836534

NORTHERN
Neil Carmichael
Recreation & Amenities
Department
George Street

North Shields
Tyne & Wear
Tel. (0632) 585085

NORTH WEST
Alan Foster
117 Mansfield Road
Ashurst
Skelmersdale
Lancashire
Tel. (0695) 23979

SOUTH EAST
Don Ferguson
30a Belitha Villas
London
N1 1PD
Tel. 01-607 2211

WEST MIDLANDS
Mrs J. Gerard-Thesingh
Flat 4, 17 Droitwich Road
Barbourne
Worcester WR3 7LG

YORKSHIRE
J. Mortimer
94 Bellhouse Way
Foxwood Lane
York YO2 3LN
Tel. (0904) 763688

SCOTLAND
Brian Parker
167 Gilmore Place
Edinburgh
Scotland
Tel. 031-228 4616

For more information on baseball in Britain, contact:

PRESIDENT
Don Smallwood
British Baseball
Federation
197 Newbridge Road
Hull HU9 2LR
Tel. (0482) 76169

NATIONAL LEAGUE COMMISSIONER
Alan Foster
117 Mansfield Road
Ashurst
Skelmersdale
Lancashire
Tel. (0695) 23979

NATIONAL LEAGUE CHIEF UMPIRE
Ted Thesingh
Flat 4, 17 Droitwich Road
Barbourne
Worcester WR3 7LG
Tel. (0905) 22622

NATIONAL LEAGUE CHIEF SCORER
Alan Kenney
62 Castlehaven Road
London NW1 8PU
Tel. 01-267 4782

NATIONAL JUNIOR BASEBALL OFFICER
Benny Benson
82 Manesty Crescent
Clifton
Nottingham
Tel. (0602) 212473

NATIONAL LEAGUE ADMINISTRATOR
Brad Thompson
Newton Works
27/29 Macklin Street
London WC2B 5LX
Tel. 01-831 6767